Cambridge Elements ≡

Elements in Shakespeare and Pedagogy
edited by
Liam E. Semler
University of Sydney
Gillian Woods
Birkbeck College, University of London

ANTI-RACIST SHAKESPEARE

Ambereen Dadabhoy
Harvey Mudd College

Nedda Mehdizadeh
University of California, Los Angeles

CAMBRIDGE
UNIVERSITY PRESS

CAMBRIDGE
UNIVERSITY PRESS

Shaftesbury Road, Cambridge CB2 8EA, United Kingdom

One Liberty Plaza, 20th Floor, New York, NY 10006, USA

477 Williamstown Road, Port Melbourne, VIC 3207, Australia

314–321, 3rd Floor, Plot 3, Splendor Forum, Jasola District Centre,
New Delhi – 110025, India

103 Penang Road, #05–06/07, Visioncrest Commercial, Singapore 238467

Cambridge University Press is part of Cambridge University Press & Assessment,
a department of the University of Cambridge.

We share the University's mission to contribute to society through the pursuit of
education, learning and research at the highest international levels of excellence.

www.cambridge.org
Information on this title: www.cambridge.org/9781009001328

DOI: 10.1017/9781009004633

First published 2023

A catalogue record for this publication is available from the British Library.

ISBN 978-1-009-00132-8 Paperback
ISSN 2632-816X (online)
ISSN 2632-8151 (print)

Anti-Racist Shakespeare

Elements in Shakespeare and Pedagogy

DOI: 10.1017/9781009004633

First published online: January 2023

Ambereen Dadabhoy
Harvey Mudd College

Nedda Mehdizadeh
University of California, Los Angeles

Author for correspondence: Ambereen Dadabhoy (dadabhoy@g.hmc.edu), Nedda Mehdizadeh (nmehdiz@ucla.edu)

ABSTRACT: *Anti-Racist Shakespeare* argues that Shakespeare is a productive site to cultivate an anti-racist pedagogy. It outlines the necessary theoretical foundations for educators to develop a critical understanding of the *longue durée* of racial formation so that they can implement anti-racist pedagogical strategies and interventions in their classrooms. This Element advances teaching Shakespeare through race and anti-racism in order to expose students to the unequal structures of power and domination that are systemically reproduced within society, culture, academic disciplines, and classrooms. The authors contend that this approach to teaching Shakespeare and race empowers students not only to see these paradigms but also to take action by challenging and overturning them. This title is also available as Open Access on Cambridge Core.

KEYWORDS: Shakespeare, race, pedagogy, anti-racism, early modern studies

ISBNs: 9781009001328 (PB), 9781009004633 (OC)

ISSNs: 2632-816X (online), 2632-8151 (print)

Contents

Introduction: Why an Anti-Racist Shakespeare?

Anti-Racist Shakespeare emerges from our individual and collective experiences as instructors of Shakespeare and Premodern Critical Race Studies (PCRS), and we see our Element intervening in these existing discussions by emphasizing the profound race-work that happens through race-attentive pedagogy. The classroom is where transformative discussions about premodern texts and their relation to contemporary racial hierarchies occur; therefore, we argue that pedagogy is central to how teachers, students, practitioners, and scholars can investigate the importance of race in Shakespeare's works. As instructors with critical investments in anti-racist and inclusive teaching methodologies, we aim to create spaces where students are exposed to theories of racial power and are equipped to develop strategies for resistance to hegemonic racial regimes. Our anti-racist pedagogy is rooted in helping students cultivate a critical vocabulary, a robust understanding of historical precedent, and a platform to share their ideas in an intellectually rigorous and supportive environment. The theoretical foundations and practical strategies we offer in *Anti-Racist Shakespeare* utilize Shakespeare and his works to convey how race and racial relations of power are present in every classroom whether instructors realize it or not. Therefore, we contend that the concepts and lessons in *Anti-Racist Shakespeare* are transferable to any discipline.

Our emphasis on race in Shakespeare pedagogy is spurred by what Peter Erickson and Kim F. Hall (2016) described as a "pathological averseness to thinking about race" in Shakespeare studies (2). In response to critics who claim that such an inquiry is anachronistic and incongruent with the field, Erickson and Hall argue that institutional and everyday resistance to scholarship on premodern constructions of race willfully ignores the evidence of racial formation in these works. This phenomenon masquerades as a desire to protect the integrity of Shakespeare by suggesting that the early modern period was void of racial distinction and by eliding the concrete ways in which European mercantile and imperial expansion led to the emergence of racial categories that would have damaging material effects on non-white, non-European peoples. Erickson and Hall offer a genealogy of scholarship that chronicles the ongoing antagonism to this method of inquiry in Shakespeare studies. As they argue, race is not external to Shakespeare: it is internally constructed within his works and, therefore, integral to disclosing the contours of Shakespeare's canon and his world. Shakespeare's works perform vital race-work, articulating a premodern grammar of race well in advance of the systematized vocabulary used today to describe the process of racial formation. Their manifesto challenges Shakespeare scholars and instructors to reconsider scholarly practices while also advocating for a material change to the field through the development of new scholarly, pedagogical, and social frameworks.

We take seriously Erickson and Hall's (2016) contention that "ignoring or disparaging race will not make it go away as a question for our – or Shakespeare's – time" (3), and in *Anti-Racist Shakespeare* we answer their call for robust change by deliberately extending the scholarship on premodern race into the arena of pedagogy. *Anti-Racist Shakespeare* suggests pedagogical practices that demonstrate how Shakespeare can be employed to develop a critical orientation toward the *longue durée* of racial thinking. This Element makes the case for teaching Shakespeare through race in order to expose students to the unequal structures of power and domination that are systemically reproduced within societies, cultures, academic disciplines, and classrooms. We argue that this critical approach to teaching Shakespeare and race empowers students not only to see these paradigms but also to challenge and overturn them.

Interrogating race in Shakespeare and disrupting racial projects in their own contemporary spheres requires that students understand how race emerges as an important knowledge and classificatory system (Hall, 2021b). Our framework follows race scholars Michael Omi and Howard Winant's (2014) concept of "racial formation," which exposes the historically contingent and unstable ways that human difference is transformed into race to support social and material systems, regimes, and hierarchies (105). Although their study focuses on contemporary racial formation in the United States, they trace its roots to European encounters with Indigenous peoples of the so-called new world, identifying race as an important "master category" of human difference in the early modern period (106). As decades of premodern race scholarship similarly argues, race was a central category in early modern social and cultural formation.

From plays like George Peele's *The Battle of Alcazar* (1591) to Philip Massinger's *The Renegado* (1624), early modern English dramatists represented the foreign on their domestic stages, exposing the allure of the so-called Other while also limning the boundaries of the self. Racial difference was key to how the Other and self were made legible, yet race was not then – as it is not now – a stable category or descriptor; it was in the process of being formed. Race as somatic and cultural difference signaled power and domination and was negotiated through these texts even as it was being discursively produced in official cultural documents, such as Elizabeth I's edicts calling for the deportation of "blackamoors" from her realm (Dadabhoy, 2021: 30–32). Early modern English racial thinking emphasized difference and Otherness, often locating those qualities in human biological or somatic variation – such as skin color – and in culture, religion, and custom, in order to stake claims of knowledge, power, and authority, which were rooted in England's nascent imperial ambitions. Within this political and social context, Shakespeare's texts perform ideological work by authorizing knowledge about race through the construction and representation of who is and is not human via forms of somatic difference.

Exposing students to the historical foundation of how race emerges as an important category of human organization gives them the tools to see how these processes operate within society. In the last several years, there have been widespread protests of police brutality and the tearing down of monuments to enslavers in what has become a global movement for racial reckoning (Gunia et al., 2021). The response has been a deep entrenchment of white anger and resentment. Popular depictions of this renewed culture war lack the critical framing and engagement to expose the long-standing social inequities historically rooted in racist ideology still affecting communities today. *Anti-Racist Shakespeare* is motivated by the world we and our students inhabit. Our study points to the centrality of race in society and the discourses that simultaneously challenge and support systemic inequity within societies founded on white supremacy.

Addressing a culturally fraught moment in the United States and the United Kingdom, where the necessity to attend to race, racial formation, and systemic racism is urgent, *Anti-Racist Shakespeare* engages with the discipline of critical race theory (CRT) as a hermeneutic. A field of legal studies, CRT centers an awareness of how racialization, particularly non-whiteness, results in social and legal outcomes that belie the abstract justness of the law. Recently, however, CRT has become a cultural flashpoint, weaponized by conservative movements to guard against critiques of historical and systemic racism. The Trump administration deemed it a "destructive ideology" (Exec. Order No. 13,950, 85 Fed. Reg. 188 [Sept. 28, 2020]) while the UK equalities minister censured it as "promoting partisan political views . . . without balance" (Turner, 2021). These ongoing attacks on CRT are not isolated; such official language reflects the prevailing Anglo-American belief in a race-neutral society, and continues to regulate whether, when, why, and how the history of racism can be taught in schools. According to this meritocratic framework, societal structures are inherently fair to all who strive for success within their domains, so long as they play by their rules. Similarly, they argue that all citizens of the United States and United Kingdom have the same rights and are therefore treated equally in society and under the law. However, CRT posits that the foundation of ideas like "human," "natural rights," and "liberalism" are flawed because race and other interlocking systems of oppression make possessing inherent rights within these systems impossible for everyone. As Derrick Bell (1995) observed, disguising racial power within the language of unraced humanity is an "abstraction, put forth as 'rational' or 'objective' truth, smuggling the privileged choice of the privileged to depersonify their claims and then pass them off as the universal authority and the universal good" (901). Attempts to critique inequities within this supposedly merito-cratic system are "oppressed, distorted, ignored, silenced, destroyed, appro-priated, commodified, and marginalized – and all of this, not accidentally" to preserve the status quo (901). As Bell predicted, de facto and de jure policies in the United States and United Kingdom have sought to discipline investigations into the historic and current manner that race and racism affect social and political beings.

Anti-Racist Shakespeare argues for a pedagogy that centers racial literacy as a necessary framework for instructors and students to critically engage with issues of race, racism, and racial formation. We have observed in our classrooms that students are eager for this instruction; their questions and comments alert us to their desire to learn how to negotiate the deep divisions that inform their lived experiences. In her groundbreaking sociological study examining families with white mothers and Black fathers, *A White Side of Black Britain*, France Winddance Twine (2010) uses the term racial literacy "to provide a theoretically grounded analysis of the ways *white* members of transracial families negotiate race, racism, and racialization and acquire racial literacy" (4). She defines racial literacy as "an analytical orientation and a set of practices that reflect shifts in perceptions of race, racism and whiteness. It is a way of perceiving and responding to racism that generates a repertoire of discursive and material practices" (92). Twine's framework uncovers how race informs every aspect of daily life, which leads to greater comprehension of the "racial codes" that circulate in society in order to develop tools to decipher and challenge them (92).

We turn to Twine in *Anti-Racist Shakespeare* because her concept of racial literacy aligns with the close reading practices of literary studies. She outlines a set of "components" that encompass what it means to be literate in race, racism, and racial formation, which include: clearly defining keywords; understanding the operations of race and racism intersectionally; recognizing the social power of whiteness; and "possess[ing] a racial grammar and vocabulary to discuss race, racism, and antiracism, and the ability to interpret racial codes and racialized practices" (Twine 2010: 92). Taken together, these "components" describe an understanding of the historical and contemporary foundations of race and offer guidance in the coded language under which racism often lurks. Twine's racial literacy framework has extended into scholarly discourse on educational practice, particularly in how racial literacy can inform methods of teaching. These studies demonstrate how becoming racially literate must begin with educating faculty in this framework so that they can instruct students on how to identify, analyze, and examine issues concerning race (Sealey-Ruiz, 2021).

Twine's racial literacy framework and its extension into education studies has likewise permeated conversations about teaching Shakespeare. For example, Ian Smith has pointed out how a lack of racial literacy facilitates the construction of white identity and subjectivity through reading practices that leave the racial character of whiteness "unmarked" (Sanchez Castillo, 2019). According to Smith, racial literacy decodes whiteness, "mak[ing] it visible, and therefore subject to reflection and critique and change" (Sanchez Castillo, 2019). In his video "Whiteness: A Primer for Understanding Shakespeare," he further notes that "white invisibility ... becomes something one has protected for a long period of time in Shakespeare studies and it prevents one from being seen. It's a strategic move, then, to somehow dismiss race from Shakespeare whether it's Blackness or whiteness because it's a way to not hav[e] to account for one's role in whiteness itself" (Smith, 2020). As long as whiteness remains invisible, discussions about race remain limited. Instructors and students need to develop a complex and sophisticated approach to race and racism as a historical and contemporary phenomenon with material power in order to apprehend its overt and covert operations and learn to decipher the codes through which it functions.

To have these rigorous conversations about race and whiteness, instructors and students must fully understand the terminology used to interrogate the complex systems of power under review. While there are several ways to define these terms, it is equally important to emphasize the asymmetrical relations of power that inform how racial hierarchies and racist systems function. Karen E. Fields and Barbara J. Fields's (2014) definition of race in *Racecraft* articulates its seemingly naturalized quality despite it being a social, rather than a biological construct: "the term *race* stands for the conception or the doctrine that nature produced humankind in distinct groups, each defined by inborn traits that its members share and that differentiate them from members of other groups of the same kind but on unequal rank" (16). Commonplace understandings of race are rooted in the physical, embodied, and phenotypic characteristics of groups, rather than in the power, domination, and subordination of those who are racialized in racist regimes (Hall, 2021b). Most people understand race as a natural, biological phenomenon when what they are really perceiving is somatic difference to which racial projects have assigned moral and cultural meaning. Therefore, while race is a social construct, which attains its power discursively, it has very real, material effects on the lives of those who are found to possess race (non-white, non-European people) and those who are perceived as not having race (white people).

Because most people possess a commonplace idea about race and racism, guiding students through a more critically robust engagement with the terminology and methodology in race studies, and its nuanced meanings, leads to better student analyses and interventions. This process begins at the level of language, ensuring that students understand that race is a system of individual and collective power. Beverley Daniel Tatum (2017) offers clear definitions and vocabulary to help readers grasp the special quality of race. She argues that, for most people, racism is used interchangeably with prejudice, which obscures the relation of unequal power that inheres in racist or race-based systems. Racism is a system of race-based advantage that benefits those with the most privilege: white, cis-gendered, heterosexual, upper-middle class, able-bodied men. Tatum's definition of racism "allows us to see that racism, like other forms of oppression, is not only a personal ideology based on racial prejudice but a *system* involving cultural messages and institutional policies and practices as well as the beliefs and actions of individuals" (87). Likewise, Eduardo Bonilla-Silva stresses the systemic power of race, arguing that racism emerges because of the unequal distribution of power and resources resulting in different outcomes for different people. He explains that

> actors in super-ordinate positions (dominant race) develop a set of social practices (a racial praxis if you will) and an ideology to maintain the advantages they receive based on their racial classification, that is, they develop a *structure* to reproduce their systemic advantages. Therefore, the foundation of racism is not the ideas that individuals may have about others, but the social edifice erected over racial inequality. (Bonilla-Silva, 2006: 24)

These explications of race and racism offer students the necessary vocabulary that moves them toward a practice of precision in language when discussing race and situates their discussions within a framework of structural inequity. Consequently, this critical engagement guides them away from reproducing analyses that are untethered to the material realities of how these systems operate.

Because so much of the focus in a certain mode of "race studies" has been to look at those identities and groups labeled non-white, the representation and racialized power of whiteness often goes unquestioned. Richard Dyer (2017) examines this seeming undetectability of whiteness, wherein he insists that the dominant culture must question the "racial imagery of white people" in their own cultural productions to understand how whiteness has come to signify "the human norm" (1). Dyer argues that whiteness is an unmentioned, unacknowledged, and unraced position; in short, white people are just people, while non-white people are raced and therefore represent the specificity and particularly of their race. Whiteness is invisible and individuated. Non-whiteness is visible and collective (2). Consequently, whiteness occupies the "powerful" (3) position of the universal, deracinated, subject. These processes enable whiteness to mask and even erase its own racial position, power, and privilege.

While Dyer asks readers to confront racial formation through the representation of whiteness in cinema, his larger argument that "there is something at stake in looking at, or continuing to ignore, white racial imagery" (1) could be applied to the academy itself, which obfuscates its own racial whiteness while continuing to deploy racial power and knowledge. In "Coloring the Past, Rewriting Our Future: RaceB4Race," Margo Hendricks reminds those new to the field of the importance of its genealogy and its critical and ethical interdisciplinary commitments. She argues,

> In this body of work, all evidence (or nearly all of the evidence) of the work done to nurture and make productive the land is ignored or briefly alluded to. In other words, the ancestry is erased. No articulation of the complex genealogy that produced Premodern Critical Race Studies exists, which in turn, drew these academic "settlers," and I am calling them "settlers," to premodern race. And just like capitalist "White settler colonialism," [this uncritical version of premodern race studies] fails to acknowledge the

scholarly ancestry – the genealogy – that continues to inhabit and nurture the critical process for the study of premodern race. (Hendricks, 2019)

Rather than discouraging interest in PCRS, Hendricks urges scholars to be wary of how academia functions, which rewards the logics of discovery. The process she identifies here is not unique to premodern studies; it is the foundation upon which the academy is established. As an institution, the academy has a mission to cultivate "excellence," and often, this idea of excellence is coded language for whiteness: a predominantly white professoriate teaches predominantly white authors in classrooms that prioritize the needs of predominantly white students. The settler-scholars who Hendricks argues have colonized scholarship on race in early modern studies – and by extension the academy – can dip in and out of stories and scholarship by and about non-white peoples because they signify authority, objectivity, and universality. This process allows the academy to continue functioning within a white imperialist framework.

As a white, European author with an imperialist fantasy of his own, Shakespeare and his works reproduce those white, European, imperialist agendas. Each of his plays enacts the consolidation of white privilege in multiple ways, including the positioning of whiteness as the ideal, as that which is most pure, as that which is most human, as that which is most familiar and recognizable to an early modern audience. The non-white racialized Others in Shakespeare's plays are purposefully made strange: they become the object of study for Shakespeare's white, European characters who are afforded the authority to classify their theatrical counterparts according not only to their physical features but also to their behavioral patterns. If teachers, students, practitioners, and scholars study Shakespeare without attending to this process, then they rehearse his imperial fantasies and legitimize this white supremacist framework by leaving it unchecked. Shakespeare's white projections of racial difference remain unquestioned as do the white desires they serve. When faculty reiterate and reinforce these positions with each Shakespeare course they teach, they cement his role as a facilitator of such fantasies within the academy. As the author assigned most frequently in literature courses, Shakespeare stands as the unquestioned authority on the human experience, which, in turn, teaches students that the idea of the human experience that he has shaped is *the* universal to which all should aspire. Teaching Shakespeare in this way is in service to white supremacy and a disservice to students.

We purposefully use the term *white supremacy* in *Anti-Racist Shakespeare* because it cuts through the abstraction of universality to the larger structure underpinning it. We follow political philosopher Charles W. Mills (1998), who pinpoints the term's "semantic virtue of clearly signaling reference to a system, a particular kind of polity, so structured as to advantage whites" (100). While neither we nor Mills claim that all political systems are white supremacist – he even specifies that the term is intended to "focus attention on the dimension of racial oppression" – early modern England and Europe did develop a race consciousness that led to the construction of race-based systems of subordination and labor. Indeed, Mills argues that "white supremacy as a *system*, or set of systems, clearly comes into existence through European expansionism and the imposition of European rule through settlement and colonialism on aboriginal and imported slave populations" (Mills, 2003: 38). We use this term to signal the larger social and political systems rooted in hierarchies that position white identities as superior to non-white identities, which justified harmful and oppressive systemic devaluation and subordination of non-white peoples, the occupation of their lands, and theft of their resources. Mobilizing the term *white supremacy* in the context of Shakespeare, then, is far from anachronistic; rather, it offers instructors and students precise language through which to excavate the historical sediments of race-based systems of power that persist today.

Attempting an anti-racist Shakespeare pedagogy requires familiarity with contemporary as well as historical understandings of race, racial formation, racial thinking, and white supremacy. Our deliberate naming of white supremacy registers the "resistant knowledge project" (Collins, 2019: 88) of anti-racist pedagogy, which mandates that we confront the root cause of racial difference and racial power. When instructors focus on the effects of non-white racialization without considering the benefits that accrue to white racialization, they are tacitly endorsing the project of white supremacy, which is invested in the obscure and elusive material construction of white racial power. The theoretical methodologies instructors employ in their Shakespeare courses must confront white supremacy head-on, and to do so, they must be interdisciplinary. Literary studies in general, and Shakespeare studies more specifically, can learn from other disciplines such as sociology, cultural studies, and education, which have all developed deep and rigorous analyses of race and white supremacy. Despite many forms of interdisciplinarity in the field, much of early modern race scholarship – particularly scholarship that does not fall under the rubric of PCRS – has used charges of "anachronism" and "American exceptionalism" to dismiss the importance of studying white supremacy. Such work has, instead, centered the presence of non-white racialized Others such as Aaron, Othello, or Shylock as representative of a limited form of inclusion in the Shakespearean canon. More perniciously, such studies have advocated for a race-neutral or racially innocent Shakespeare and early modern period, absolving the era and its writers from complicity in its emerging racialized ideologies within an array of literary and cultural productions.

Anti-racist pedagogy is an antidote to the epistemology of whiteness that undergirds such teaching practices. Rooted in the work of CRT and education theory, anti-racist pedagogy centers race as constitutive to the asymmetrical relations of power, domination, and subordination within societies based on racial hierarchies, like the United States and the United Kingdom. By focusing on race, racism, and racial formation as foundational to the operations of these societies, anti-racist pedagogy reveals and challenges the systemic operations of white supremacy and white privilege within academic disciplines and within institutions (Kishimoto, 2018: 541). Anti-racist pedagogy commits to interrogating race, yet it is also intersectional, paying close attention to the multiple axes of oppression that marginalized identity categories, such as sex, sexuality, gender, religion, ability, and class, can and do experience within dominant white, heterosexist, patriarchal social structures. Because anti-racist pedagogy is heavily influenced by the groundbreaking work of Paulo Freire (1970) and his commitment to education as a tool for the liberation of the oppressed, it is an emancipatory practice that awakens critical consciousness in our students, specifically around the issues of racial injustice and the destructive material effects of racist and racially structured societies. Anti-racist pedagogy, then, is a resistant knowledge project that comprises a critical orientation and practice that can effect social transformation and liberation for students and instructors (Collins, 2019: 87–97).

Part of our method in *Anti-Racist Shakespeare* is to destabilize Shakespeare's universality through the framework of racial literacy and to shake up Shakespeare's position as *the* author of *the* human condition. Whether students have subscribed to or inherited the myth of Shakespeare's universality, he has long enjoyed a dominant position in the academy, in the theater, and in Anglo-American culture at large. It is his oeuvre that is so often assigned on course syllabi, staged for devoted audiences, and quoted in a variety of venues. Despite his ubiquity, however, his works are not necessarily *relevant* to the lives of those who read his plays and poems. In fact, many of our students are harmed by the dangerous racializing of characters and personae in Shakespeare's texts. Worse, they have internalized the expectation to relate to Shakespeare because of his universality. This experience can be traumatizing for students who observe the villainization of characters with whom they share identites and witness their dehumanization in service of advancing the fantasy of the ideal white subject, even as their instructors insist on Shakespeare's deep awareness of the universal human experience. Assuming Shakespeare's universality leaves little space – if any – for students to engage with the larger process of race-work in Shakespeare, alienating those students whose histories and lived experiences are demonized by the canon.

We propose an alternative to the paradigm of relevance and, instead, offer that of *salience*. The notion of relevance requires students to meet the text where *it* is as a fixed expression of human experience. Instead, we ask that our students examine that which "leaps" (*OED*, salient, adj. and n.) from the page as distinctive and prominent in the Shakespearean text, giving them the freedom to identify what is made important to them through their focused inquiry. This analytical process, then, affords students the opportunity to investigate the ideas and principles animating the text and to engage in dynamic discussions about early modern racial formation and its long-lasting effects. Such reorientation toward salience can empower students to see relevance from a new perspective, to see themselves – not in Shakespeare's words – but in the work that Shakespeare does on the consumers of his legacy. It is through this experience that both white and non-white students can understand their relationship to Shakespeare, to the academy, and to larger structures of power in society.

Anti-Racist Shakespeare is an interdisciplinary study that seeks to expand scholarly discussions about Shakespeare and race, specifically locating this subfield within the realm of education and teaching practices. Our approach is to provide a theoretically informed pedagogy that seeks to reorient educators toward a new and urgent perspective on teaching Shakespeare. While this Element presents specific suggestions that educators can take into the classroom, the critical work we undertake here is to offer instructors a deeper context for the issues that cohere around race, racism, racial formation, white supremacy, and anti-racism to shift the instructional paradigm and reframe the Shakespeare course from its foundations. Because our aim is to reexamine the underpinnings of the discipline and how instructors teach within it, the teaching strategies we offer in *Anti-Racist Shakespeare* can be utilized in a variety of courses, from lower- and upper-division undergraduate classes, to courses for non-majors, to graduate student instruction, and to courses that study other canonical authors. We contend that addressing this orientation toward Shakespeare from its roots will help facilitate the application of strategic methods that assist students in developing racial literacy and becoming conversant with Shakespeare and the issues that attend to race.

We begin to address these foundations in Section 1, "Shakespeare's Racial Invisibility," which outlines how Shakespeare's invisible whiteness underpins both English departments and Shakespeare's monumental status within the field. By acknowledging Shakespeare as a raced figure who benefits from whiteness and whose work engages in race-making, educators can guide students toward a significant understanding of how race operates in Shakespeare's works. In Section 2, "Conceptualizing and Designing an Anti-Racist Shakespeare Course," we argue that an awareness of Shakespeare's whiteness can help instructors develop courses with an anti-racist orientation. We suggest that designing the course with Shakespeare's privilege in mind influences the specific texts instructors will include on syllabi, the projects they will assign, and how they will train their students to read and interpret texts. Section 3, "Building Shakespearean Communities," explores how a Shakespeare course that centers the needs of its students and adopts a community-based approach to education will help instructors navigate the complex terrain of teaching Shakespeare and race proactively. Finally, Section 4, "The Salience of Shakespeare," argues that students' developing racial literacy skills in the anti-racist Shakespeare classroom can influence how Shakespeare is salient to their lived experiences. We focus on how they can utilize racial literacy to "read" race and to "read" Shakespeare in and beyond the space of the classroom. This application of lessons and skills demonstrates students' command of the material in significant ways, particularly when it comes to enacting social change. Each section in *Anti-Racist Shakespeare* concludes with a Teaching Vignette and a Teacher Reflection, offering instructors lessons that they can take into their classrooms and the opportunity to reflect on their pedagogy as well as the specific themes and topics of each section. We invite readers of this Element to use these teaching reflections interactively, by setting responses to writing, using the guiding questions as prompts for discussion among peers, or utilizing other formats to critically examine the work they are undertaking for themselves and with their students. We also encourage readers to revisit these prompts and their responses as their pedagogy evolves, because developing an anti-racist pedagogy is an ongoing process.

Writing an Element about anti-racist Shakespeare pedagogy has meant that we, the authors, have reflected deeply on our own positionality in relation to both Shakespeare and race. As two women from non-English, non-European, and non-white cultures, we have personal experience of being marginalized in and by the English and Shakespearean canon and in the social, political, and cultural systems in which we reside. We are also educators whose teaching and research focus on contemporary and early modern race and racial formation. Moreover, our critical orientation toward this topic is shaped by our social locations, by which we mean the factors that position us in society such as race, gender, age, ability, citizenship, sexuality, and religion. Who we are affects what we study, and how. Indeed, as Edward Said (2003) outlines in *Orientalism*, "no one has ever devised a method for detaching the scholar from the circumstances of life, from the fact of his involvement (conscious or unconscious) with a class, a set of beliefs, a social position, or from the mere activity of being a member of a society. These continue to bear on what he does professionally" (10). Our social locations inform our scholarship and teaching; in fact, they can sometimes facilitate different ways of seeing because of the experience of marginalization or non-belonging to the dominant group (hooks, 1992: 115–32).

We rehearse the importance of social locations because non-white racialized instructors of Shakespeare – whose identities challenge the normative whiteness of academia, English departments, and Shakespeare studies – often have an extra hurdle to overcome (Dadabhoy, 2020a: 3). Commenting on the pervasive whiteness of the field, Dennis A. Britton aptly remarks, "not everyone who works on Shakespeare gets to be considered a Shakespearean" (Britton, 2018: 227). Despite the presumed universality of our author, practitioners of Shakespeare in theater and the academy remain overwhelmingly white as do the common perceptions of who can legitimately "do" Shakespeare. Therefore, how we are perceived – by our students and our colleagues – informs whether we are considered qualified to teach and write about Shakespeare. These are the invisible and unmarked workings of race that structure the field, the knowledge it generates, and the people it validates as authorities over it. Race as whiteness is the marker of inclusion into Shakespeare and early modern studies. Thus, all instructors, whether they are white or non-white, must reflect on and question how their social locations allow them certain forms of authority and power over Shakespeare and on the kind of knowledge and power they can exert over investigations into race, racism, racial formation, and anti-racism.

In our own investigation into anti-racist approaches to Shakespeare, we consider salient what Shakespeare can tell us about how power works and how dominant regimes operate. Like us, our students are affected by the moment in which they live, the way that race is constitutive of their reality and salient to how they function in society. For this reason, we resist the assertion that asking students to think about racialized power in Shakespeare's texts might be seen as politicizing our classrooms. The classroom is *already* political because it is a space where power inheres and is consistently negotiated. The structure of the classroom, regardless of how instructors might want to decentralize power, is hierarchical by virtue of the qualifications, knowledge, authority, and experience they hold. Educators can, however, share power by acknowledging the experience and other forms of knowledge and expertise that students bring to the classroom that can and should inform instructors' interpretive practices. Further, instructors who occupy non-white bodies have racial identities that speak for them and communicate information to students without the instructors' permission. The convenient fiction of a neutral, depoliticized classroom, then, excuses repudiating the task of anti-racist pedagogy. Our aim here is neither to bully the Bard nor to "indoctrinate" our students, but rather to offer a corrective for the presiding academic agenda that insists on the normative hegemony of whiteness as a frame that controls the authors that instructors assign and the material they teach on course syllabi, such as Shakespeare's works. An anti-racist pedagogical approach highlights the way race structures society, giving students a broader understanding of these systems through a cultivation of racial literacy.

Though students may express discomfort with engaging the topic of race, it is more often the case that they respond with eagerness when examining Shakespeare's texts within this framework. Students are well informed about the world in which they live, but they want to be guided through these complex histories and systems to communicate effectively about timely issues with a better grasp of the underlying politics of course material. When instructors teach Shakespeare as part of the status quo by neglecting to intervene in the work his plays and poems do to construct and consolidate forms of racial injustice, they further circumscribe for students the kind of intellectual inquiry for which they are eager. Instructors let students down by not answering their call for an informed and meaningful engagement with this material. *Anti-Racist Shakespeare* seeks to disrupt this process by promoting a racially-attentive examination of early modern literature and Shakespeare in order to empower students to read the racial contours of Shakespeare's world as well as their own.

Teaching Vignette

Othello, THE Race Play

When we think about Shakespeare and race, the obvious example is always *Othello*. The play has become *the* go-to text for scholars, teachers, and practitioners on the topic of race and racism in Shakespeare. We begin our study of anti-racist Shakespeare pedagogy with this play precisely because of its outsized and overdetermined influence, which trespasses the boundaries of academic study into the popular representation of Black people and Black masculinity. As Ben Okri (2015) notes, "in three centuries of Othello committing murder and suicide on the stage no significant change in attitude towards black people has occurred" (64). The play's message on race – as incoherent as it might be – is certainly not racial harmony. To teach *Othello* in the context of teaching race might seem appropriate, but instructors should always be cautious of what they are, in fact, teaching about race through this play.

Our aim in this section is to unsettle the perspective that teaching race requires the presence of a Black or other non-white racialized character. While we do not deny that Othello's Blackness is important or that it elicits race consciousness in other characters and in audiences, we want to trouble the reading and interpretive practices that make race visible and meaningful only through the presence of non-whiteness. Such practices maintain the slipperiness of whiteness while attempting to fix or stabilize race in non-whiteness. Rather than yielding to the invisibility of whiteness within white dominant epistemologies, we insist on noting the importance of white as a raced category. Our teaching of *Othello* demonstrates the processes of racial formation by attending to the ways in which the hypervisibility of the Black body allows for the invisibility of whiteness. Thus, our pedagogy with *Othello* seeks to flip the script and focus on the dominant racialized power of whiteness in the play.

The action of *Othello* is problematic because it presents irreconcilable ideas about the relation of Othello's character to his racial designation. The problem of the play is that it does not understand what to do with its hero or his race because of its own racial investments in whiteness. In other words, the isolation Othello endures because of his racial difference animates the plot and allows Iago's schemes to succeed; however, his status as tragic hero depends on his inability to conform to the whiteness of his social milieu. Othello is doomed from the start because his race "is the cause" (5.2.1) of his and the play's bloody outcome. Highlighting the race trap of this play frees readers from questions about whether the play is racist and moves them toward readings that probe the machinations of race-making and the ends to which race is mobilized to do the state of whiteness "some service" (5.2.355). Our approach to *Othello* as a play with a race problem – that is, its depiction of the incommensurability of Blackness within a culture beginning to consolidate its own identity around various forms of whiteness – presents new ways for students to understand the play's fraught racial dynamics.

Flipping the script on *Othello* to focus on whiteness still requires a critical examination of Blackness, because whiteness articulates itself and secures its boundaries and borders through difference. However, by putting the focus on the forging of whiteness and white patriarchal domination in the play, instructors can facilitate student interpretations and analyses that locate the various systems of subordination upon which the social world of the play relies. Moreover, they can underscore for students the shared and different oppressions experienced by characters because of their social locations. We offer an "entry point" (Thompson and Turchi, 2016: 23) into the play through its first scene, a close reading of which guides students toward an understanding of race that focuses on the way whiteness works.

The first scene in *Othello* establishes the play's racial foundation through its demonization and dehumanization of Blackness, which tacitly forge the opposite qualities in whiteness. It gives Iago total epistemological control to fabricate Othello in the minds of Desdemona's outraged father, Brabantio, and most crucially, the audience, using lurid sexual imagery to suture Othello's Blackness to degeneracy and bestiality. Pausing on this scene to consider the ideological race-work it performs in constructing whiteness offers students the opportunity to read against the grain of Iago's intentions and to apply this method to other moments in the text; moreover, it helps them cultivate a critical reading practice that Black feminist scholar bell hooks (1992) has labeled "the oppositional gaze." Particularly rooted in the experience of Black life under white supremacist regimes, hooks's text argues that Black people have had to cultivate resistant "looking relations" and that Black women specifically have developed a political gaze that looks from the margins because their identities and subjectivities have no place in the sexist-patriarchal regime of the traditional white male gaze (116–22). The oppositional gaze is one that deliberately refuses identification with dominant regimes of power that seek to coerce subjects into social relations that reinforce the status quo. Instructors can encourage students to participate in such resistant reading practices through targeted close readings of this scene. This perspective can help them interrogate the strategic uses of Othello's Black racial difference by white characters like Iago and Brabantio, who reinforce the cultural dominance of whiteness.

By demonstrating specific techniques of close reading, instructors can model against-the-grain reading practices for students. In addition to asking them to look for patterns and rhetorical devices, instructors can ask students to mark every instance of language that connotes or denotes race or racial status. After taking notes on that usage, students (individually or in pairs) mark the information that is being conveyed through that racialized language. For example, they can note whether the language indicating moral failure or sexual excess relates to the construction of racialized identity. Once they have compiled this data, students search for markers of white racialized identity. Because there is a decided lack of that information in this scene, students can speculate on this invisibility and examine the differences between whiteness as race and Blackness as race by considering questions such as:

- What strategies does Shakespeare employ in this scene to maintain white racial invisibility?
- How does Venetian racial invisibility shore up Othello's difference?
- How does whiteness, as a frame, organize power on the stage?

As students engage more deeply with the racial politics of the play, they might note that the invisibility of Iago's whiteness is not the only important structuring device of the scene. Rather, students can investigate what it means to have three white men – Iago, Roderigo, and Brabantio – discuss the sexuality of a Black man in racialized terms. This examination reveals how race as non-whiteness works in the dominant culture to render the whiteness of the Venetian characters invisible, thereby granting them the authority to assign meaning to Othello's body and imagined behavior. By devoting time to this scene, students begin to understand racial visibility and invisibility. The methodical practice of reading the opening of *Othello* with students models interpretive practices that question commonplace assumptions that race only inheres in non-whiteness. Students can further apply such targeted, race-attentive close reading practices to other moments in the play, for example, in 3.3 when Othello capitulates to Iago's influence, in 4.3 when Desdemona compares her life with that of her mother's Black maid, Barbary, and in 5.2 when Desdemona's fair beauty disturbs Othello's plan to kill her. An early focus on whiteness offers against-the-grain readings of the usual treatment of race in the play and makes explicit the dominating power of whiteness and white cultural supremacy.

Teacher Reflection

We end each section by asking teachers to reflect on their pedagogy as it relates to the topic of the section. In this section, we examine the importance of anti-racist pedagogy in the Shakespeare classroom. We offered a theoretical framework that not only informs our work but also acts as a primer on Shakespeare and race for our readers. For this "Teacher Reflection," we invite you to consider what anti-racism means to you and your pedagogy:

- What compels you toward an anti-racist Shakespeare pedagogy?
- What concerns you about approaching an anti-racist teaching practice?
- What skills and lessons do you already possess that prepare you for this work?
- What skills and lessons will you hone as you embark on this exploration?
- How do you think your students and colleagues will respond to your commitment to this work?

These reflective questions about cultivating an anti-racist pedagogy are meant to help teachers examine potential intellectual and affective blocks to developing an anti-racist pedagogy. By responding to these questions, whether in solitude or in community with others, in written, oral, or conceptual formats, teachers may feel discomfort about employing anti-racist strategies. We hope that creating this reflective space for teachers encourages them to approach anti-racist pedagogical practice with a deeper understanding of systemic racism, an awareness of their feelings about these unequal systems, and an openness to continue exploring this new and difficult challenge.

1 Shakespeare's Racial Invisibility

When students are taught Shakespeare's works either in secondary or post-secondary education, they are not usually encouraged to think of him as a white writer whose works address race as whiteness. Despite being a white Englishman born in the sixteenth century whose plays are now taught in English classrooms, his work has successfully been severed from his personal and political identity through the idea of Shakespearean universality. Shakespeare, the man, has been transformed into the immortal and disembodied "Bard," who metonymically stands for and as his plays and poems. Thus, the work, not the man, speaks to us "for all time," as his friend and contemporary Ben Jonson eulogized. The problem with such transcendent and universal framing, however, is that it elides the local particularity of Shakespeare, and it allows both him and his work to escape the processes of racialization in which his work is deeply imbricated and implicated. In this section we put pressure on Shakespeare's racial invisibility by yoking it to the ways in which whiteness remains racially unremarked upon in white dominant cultures. We will further expose how the "white racial frame" (Feagin, 2020) disrupts attempts at getting students to see the operations of race when located in white identity. Identifying the white racial frame improves students' racial literacy, which, as we defined in our Introduction, is the process of decoding the functions of race in commonplace discourse and action. Therefore, *Anti-Racist Shakespeare* advocates for cultivating racial literacy in students that not only helps them recognize and read race, but also critically interrogate the assumptions that obtain in normative understandings of Shakespearean whiteness as an invisible, unraced position.

One of the reasons why Shakespeare's position in the academy is unraced is because courses on Shakespeare are usually housed in English departments. National literatures, as Toni Morrison (2019) has elucidated, are artifacts that transmit the moral, aesthetic, social, and cultural values of a nation (161–97). English literature, however, occupies a special position because it signifies both a national literature (the literature of the English nation) and a linguistic tradition (literature written in English); therefore, Shakespeare can be both the fountainhead of the English nation, as he is sometimes positioned, and the most sublime poet and playwright of the English language. Given the global scope of the British Empire, English has superseded the boundaries of England's geography to become the language of both global commerce and global culture (Viswanathan, 2014). The global primacy of English uplifts Shakespeare, placing him at the pinnacle of achievement in that language and de-emphasizing his whiteness. The arrangements of English departments often designate certain courses to identify the subject positions and social locations of the writers and geographies that produced them, so that World literature and Third World literature courses sit (un)easily beside the British literature and American literature sequences in course catalogues. The former courses are geographically, imperially, and racially marked, while those that comprise "traditional" national literatures are only marked by the defining characteristics of the privileged national culture that invisibly signal all forms of belonging, including language and race. While the standard English or American literature course may include preeminent or token writers of color, they often maintain overwhelming and unacknowledged whiteness in their epistemological and aesthetic orientations, which is an assumption of whiteness that underwrites its unmarked position.

Moreover, if national literatures, housed in English departments under the aegis of English and American literatures, are the repositories of the dominant culture and values of the nation, then the canon is the sacred body of works that transmits these national ideologies. This sacral positioning of the canon obfuscates the real fact that it is deliberately designed according to specific standards and aesthetic values. The canon of English literature is particularly white, male, and elite; therefore, it speaks to a particular identity that is raced, gendered, and classed among other categories of subjectification. We are not casting aspersions upon any one or all of these identity markers, but rather making transparent who speaks for "humanity" within the English canon. Obscuring the identities of canonical writers or making them subservient or irrelevant to their aesthetic genius, reproduces the universality of white maleness at the same time that it erases its racial and gendered positions. So, too, does this occur with Shakespeare, whose place in the canon seems unshakable because the canon is constructed around him. Shakespeare *is* the canon of English literature. Proof of this can be found in debates about the construction of an educational curriculum in one of England's former colonies, where a proposal to excise Shakespeare became a matter of national concern (Thiong'o, 2005: 89–97). Shakespeare's social power regularly manifests in anxieties about his marginalization in the curriculum to make way for one that is more inclusive (Anderson, 2015). Therefore, Shakespeare's plays and poems not only represent the best that has been thought and said in the English language – to paraphrase Matthew Arnold – but also represent the telos of Englishness: they contain it (Arnold, 1869: 190).

The aim of anti-racist Shakespeare pedagogy is not to undermine the aesthetic value of Shakespeare's works; instead, it seeks to disrupt the notion that the aesthetic is not imbricated in relations of race, gender, and class, and to critique the cultural capital that accrues to Shakespeare. *Anti-Racist Shakespeare* exposes the visible and invisible operations of race within Shakespeare's works, to show how they are complicit in early modern racial formations that constructed a normative, hegemonic whiteness located in elite, white, male bodies. Because anti-racist pedagogy is also intersectional, we investigate the representation of white womanhood, which as Kim F. Hall (1995) has argued, was vital to the discourses of English imperial ambitions because they yoked white women's fairness not only to their desirability but also to the preservation of family through dynastic marriage alliances (22–23). Thus, while the white women in Shakespeare's plays are often oppressed under forms of patriarchal tyranny, they simultaneously acquire and maintain status through their literal whiteness, which they can exchange for power within heterosexual unions. *Anti-Racist Shakespeare*, then, is attentive to the many, multiple, and interlocking systems of power operating within Shakespeare's works and within academia that keep his oeuvre from being implicated within these frameworks of domination and subordination.

The cultural and institutional preservation of Shakespeare's racial invisibility offers one manifestation of the white racial frame. According to whiteness studies scholar Joe R. Feagin (2020), the "white racial frame" is "an organized set of racialized ideas, stereotypes, emotions, and inclinations used to discriminate," which simultaneously promotes a "positive orientation to whites and whiteness and a negative orientation to racial 'others'" who are exploited and oppressed" (19). Within the realm of literary studies and Shakespeare, the white racial frame can signal a "conceptual and interpretive scheme that shapes and channels assessments" (22) of plots and characters, be they white or non-white racialized people. One of the most important and pernicious maneuvers of the white racial frame is its aggressive promotion of narratives that depict "a positive view of white superiority, virtue, and moral goodness" (26). The white racial frame is both commonplace and insidious: it does not draw attention to itself. Therefore, it is an epistemology that obfuscates how it makes knowledge and meaning. As Feagin points out,

> [m]uch of the social terrain of [the United States] is signifi-
> cantly racialized. Most major institutional and geographical
> spaces, acceptable societal norms, acceptable societal roles,
> privileged language forms, preferred sociopolitical thinking,
> and favored understandings of history are white-generated,
> white-shaped, white-imposed, and/or white authenticated.
> All people, whether they are defined socially as white or not
> white, live largely within a substantially white-determined
> environment. (Feagin, 2006: 47)

We extend this "white-determined environment" to both the status of Shakespeare as a monument to the English language and its aesthetic achievement and, crucially, to the way Shakespeare has been read, taught, and performed within Anglo-American institutions.

The white racial frame is both an orientation (inclination) and an epistemology (way of knowing) that is invested in the superiority of whiteness in all social and cultural arenas. The epistemic dimension of white supremacy is vitally important because it determines what we know and how we know it. White supremacy flourishes through various and studied forms of white ignorance, through the disavowal of knowledge about racism and its effects both within our society and within the academy, in English departments, and in Shakespeare courses. White ignorance furthers the white racial frame in its refusal to see and acknowledge that frame while simultaneously centering that frame as the only one through which legitimate (white) knowledge is produced (Applebaum, 2019). Racial ignorance, as José Medina (2017) aptly claims, "is a luxury that oppressed subjects typically cannot have," because "racially oppressed subjects have no option but to master the dominant perspectives of privileged groups that shape the social world" (251). Thus, white ignorance paradoxically becomes a position of power through which white people can disclaim critical knowledge about people of color and their lives under white supremacy, and maintain a position of racial innocence (Applebaum, 2010).

Racial ignorance and innocence are the province of whiteness because the white racial frame allows for such freedoms. Barbara Applebaum (2019) argues that "[w]hite ignorance functions to mystify the consequences of unjust systems that systemically marginalized groups endure so that those who benefit from the system do not have to consider their complicity in perpetuating them" (30). By ignoring the powerful systems that contribute to the marginalization of non-white racialized people, white people can adopt a position of racial innocence because they are not personally involved in upholding those systems, even as they benefit from them. The key ideas here are the ways that racial ignorance promotes racial innocence and how both affective locations are also epistemological locations. They are about what one knows and does not know about how race works in society, or more accurately, they are about "willful ignorance," a deliberate position of not knowing that helps "the dominant group have a *vested interest in not knowing*" (30). This "vested interest" actively works to "safeguard white moral innocence while at the same time shielding unjust systems from contestation" (30). In the circular workings of white supremacy and its epistemological hold on the white imaginary, white people are protected from both their knowledge of and privilege in the racial hierarchy, which, in turn, allows this hierarchy to smoothly function without internal challenges. The racial hierarchy, then, is a social, legal, and political structure as well as an epistemological one. What people know and how they know it is implicated within racial and racist regimes in addition to their own social locations within those systems.

Returning to Shakespeare, we want to explore how his works *and* the ways in which they have been studied have contributed to or challenged the dominant constructions of race and racialization in our world. We are not, here, traversing the familiar territory of whether race was a significant taxonomy in the early modern period. That question has already been asked and answered (Erickson & Hall, 2016: 4). Our aim, rather, is to consider how a "racially insensitive" (Medina, 2017: 249–50) Shakespeare pedagogy advances and benefits the white racial frame or the white/right way of reading Shakespeare. By eschewing discussions of race in the classroom or confining those discussions to Shakespeare's so-called race plays (*Titus Andronicus*, *The Merchant of Venice*, *Othello*, *Antony and Cleopatra*, and *The Tempest*), instructors are not only marking an "Other" space for race within the Shakespearean canon, but also leaving unquestioned the positioning of whiteness within these same "race plays." Race becomes the remit of non-whiteness; moreover, such pedagogy deftly excludes race from being pertinent to or informing other intellectual activities undertaken in Shakespeare courses.

By strategically making the space for race through non-whiteness, instructors are eliding the significance of whiteness as a racial position. The maneuver to make non-whiteness hypervisible and whiteness invisible is the disturbing paradox of race-neutral pedagogy. In this formulation, race is an important category for analysis only when non-white characters are present, and when those characters are present, the only important thing about them is their racialized status. Such racial calculus uncovers how non-whiteness limits interpretive and intellectual possibilities and never questions the unlimited capacity that it simultaneously endows to whiteness. It reveals, as Dyer (2017) argues, the "powerful position" of whiteness, which articulates a "claim to power [that] is the claim to speak for the commonality of humanity. Raced people can't do that – they can only speak for their race. But non-raced people can, for they do not represent the interest of a race" (2). If Shakespeare pedagogy is only attentive to race as non-whiteness, then it is "racially insensitive," because it refuses to acknowledge the way whiteness works in Shakespearean texts and the broader culture (Medina, 2017: 249). It supports the dominant group's interests in either not knowing or willfully obscuring their own racialized social locations.

Anti-racist Shakespeare pedagogy actively addresses and combats this erasure by cultivating racial literacy in educators and students. Ian Smith (2020) adroitly points out that the forms of Blackness that we encounter in

Shakespeare are "produced by white culture." What Smith signals here is not only that the representation of Black identity and the ideas freighted onto that identity are white-made and manufactured, but also that these texts do not offer any kind of truth about Blackness. Rather, they present insight into white ideologies about Blackness and help us to understand how whiteness needs Blackness to articulate itself. White bodies come to have value and whiteness comes into being in concert with assigning other, lesser forms of value and limitations onto Blackness (Smith, 2020). Classroom conversations about race, then, must be attuned to how this representation is a product of and serves the white imaginary. Any truth claims about these identities must be tempered by an awareness of the way whiteness works in constructing and structuring this representation. This knowledge is especially important in Shakespeare courses because of Shakespeare's universal positioning and the benevolent and liberal ways in which educators and students are encouraged to think of him as being able to speak to and for the human condition.

To disrupt Shakespeare's position as the author of an unraced human condition, instructors must offer students the necessary hermeneutical skills that make apparent the epistemic operations of race. Smith notes that making whiteness "visible" is one way to advance students' racial literacy because "white invisibility has been practiced for a long time and it prevents whiteness from being seen" (Smith, 2020). Put another way, racial literacy is about cultivating a sensitivity and awareness of the overt and covert ways in which race and racial power organize understandings of literary texts, particularly Shakespeare. Smith (2020) foregrounds the urgency of racial literacy for students not only because of this fraught moment of racial reckoning, but also because racial literacy is a vital tool that can help reformulate Shakespeare, to question "why Shakespeare now?" To help students understand how race as whiteness works in these texts, instructors need to give them the interpretive methodologies and tools that will facilitate their investigations and analyses. Interrogating race is a specialized activity, similar to close reading, where instructors ask students to identify rhetorical devices and tropes to supplement and support their textual interpretations. Because race is discursively constructed, as Stuart Hall has shown, literary scholars are perfectly situated to help students see the connection between discourse and systems of power (Hall, 2021b: 361). Shakespearean objects are discourses that produce ideas about normative identities and hegemonic subjects: they articulate ways of seeing and being that can challenge or subvert the status quo and its dominant ideologies. Instructors can extend students' interpretive skills to include racial literacy by giving them the vocabulary about race, racism, racial power, racial marking or hypervisibility, and racial invisibility to help them more fully recognize the salience of race not only in their Shakespeare courses, but also in the societies in which they live.

Teaching Vignette

The Uses and Abuses of Shakespeare, or "Shakespeare in the Wild"

In this section, we turn from the theoretical dimension of whiteness and its relation to Shakespeare and Shakespeare studies to practical applications. We offer an assignment we call "Shakespeare in the Wild," wherein students locate how Shakespeare's cultural capital is mobilized in the realms of politics and popular culture. The purpose of this assignment is to encourage students to make explicit the racial underpinnings of these deployments. The archive of "Shakespeare in the Wild" that students will consult can be material that they find on their own or it might be curated by the instructor. Regardless of the method, students' primary task will be to exhibit their own racial literacy in decoding the white racial frame through which these representations are constructed and presented. Some guiding questions that instructors can ask their students to consider when evaluating their "Shakespeare in the Wild" resources include,

- Who is speaking?
- What kind of race-logics are guiding the representation?
- What are the structures of power already informing the use of Shakespeare?
- Why is Shakespeare here? What work is Shakespeare doing in this appearance?
- What is his cultural capital supporting or authorizing?

- What can you understand about this moment by centering race – not just Shakespeare's race but also that of the speaker?
- Who is silenced, ignored, or erased in this instance?

Shakespeare is a cultural monument, particularly in the political sphere where quotations and citations mobilize his cultural capital and historical heft. In the Anglo-American political arena this citationality is de rigueur. For example, on September 14, 2020, Texas Republican senator Ted Cruz issued a tweet in response to an announcement from the English department at the University of Chicago, which stated that for the 2020–21 graduate admissions cycle, they would only accept applicants whose work centered on Black studies, broadly construed. Cruz's tweet read: "The University of Chicago English Dept announced that, for 2 yrs [sic], it is ONLY accepting graduate applications for Black Studies. READ posting below. The following areas of study are presumably not acceptable: Shakespeare, Chaucer, Milton, Dickens, Austen" (@tedcruz, September 14, 2020). Cruz misunderstands how graduate admissions procedures work and dismisses the entire field of Black studies. As many of the responses to his tweet indicate, the field of Black studies, in fact, encompasses the white, European authors that Cruz lists as being in danger of being excised from syllabi. Based on the framing of his message, it is reasonable to conclude that Cruz is either unaware of the body of work associated with the authors he wishes to safeguard from imagined obscurity or that he *is* aware but has willfully disregarded it in service of drumming up support from his conservative base. Regardless of Cruz's intentions, the tweet relies on Shakespeare's whiteness and traffics in racial dog whistles to promote cultural antagonisms toward both higher education and Black studies. The racist coding that Cruz uses is not subtle, yet by framing it as an issue of preserving the English canon against an insurgent discipline explicitly invested in race studies, Cruz manages to make the interests of whiteness known.

The tendency for politicians in the United States to one-up their rivals through Shakespeare in times of contention is mirrored by politicians in the United Kingdom. For instance, news outlets reported that former prime minister Boris Johnson compared himself to Othello and his former aide-turned-critic Dominic Cummings to Iago after Cummings spoke to the press about Johnson's repeated disregard of lockdown regulations during the COVID-19 isolation period in May 2020 (Wilcock, 2022). Johnson's reference to *Othello* does some work for him: by tethering himself to Shakespeare, he elevates his status both in terms of imagined intimacy with Shakespeare and as someone who extends Shakespeare's tradition of white authority. Ironically, his analogy puts him in the position of Shakespeare's Black protagonist while Cummings plays the role of the conniving white villain. This orientation not only positions him as the victim – in this case, a victim to someone else's influence – but also oversimplifies Othello's plight by deracinating him. Johnson's false equivalency between the betrayal he feels and the racism Othello experiences, which destroys his life and that of his wife, exposes Johnson's lack of racial literacy and subsequent race-neutral approach to Shakespeare.

Given that Shakespeare abounds in politics, the question that emerges in this assignment is, why? Why do American and British politicians turn to Shakespeare to score political points that resonate with their constituents? By having students consider this question, instructors help them understand the long historical connection between the United States and the United Kingdom through fantasies of empire, which they mobilize through a shared language to maintain the racial system as it is. What these examples further reveal is how the United States has inherited a white, elite, and imperial tradition of Shakespeare from the United Kingdom. By analyzing these moments through the framework of racial literacy and by looking for whiteness, students can make these systems of power and domination visible. Students will want to consider how Shakespeare's whiteness precludes non-white and non-European audiences from the associations and intimacies with Shakespeare that both Cruz and Johnson rely upon in their appeals. They will further want to interrogate how "Shakespeare in the Wild" can secure Shakespeare for whiteness and from the encroachment of non-white racialized Others.

Teacher Reflection

We end each section by asking teachers to reflect on their pedagogy as it relates to the topic of the section. In this section, we examine how white invisibility operates in the study of Shakespeare and in academia. We focused on the epistemological effects of white supremacy which include the white racial frame, white ignorance, and white innocence. For this "Teacher Reflection," we invite you to consider your social location as a teacher and a person in the world:

- How do you think your social position within these power structures impacts your teaching?
- In what explicit or implicit ways have you contributed to encouraging the invisibility of whiteness in your classroom?
- What strategies might you develop to address the explicit or implicit participation you described in the previous question?
- What affective responses might emerge from being asked to consider these questions about complicity?
- How might you use your experience reflecting on these questions to support your students when they encounter these ideas?

These reflective questions about social location and the structural invisibility of whiteness are meant to help teachers examine how race and racism impact their personal and professional lives. By responding to these questions, whether in solitude or in community with others, in written, oral, or conceptual formats, teachers might feel discomfort associated with their social locations. We hope that creating this reflective space for teachers encourages them to examine the extent of their own privilege or potential racial insensitivities with curiosity and motivation to dismantle these systems.

2 Conceptualizing and Designing an Anti-Racist Shakespeare Course

Anti-racist course design requires that instructors reorient their position to Shakespeare and race in the classroom through a perspective rooted in anti-racist praxis. Some instructors of Shakespeare or English literature find implementing such practices challenging because they feel limited by what they have expertise in or whether they have institutional support to do this work. Giving into such limitations tacitly supports institutional hierarchies because instructors' affiliation within these same fields and institutions makes them complicit in exclusionary structures unless they actively engage in counter-hegemonic practices. The interpretive tools of racial literacy – particularly those that help instructors and students perceive the racial power of whiteness as we outlined in the previous section – make explicit the repertoire of racial power structures that inform Shakespeare studies. This reorientation is necessary not because instructors intend to cause harm or are operating in bad faith, but because they have been trained in fields that fundamentally obfuscate the underpinnings of white supremacy within the knowledge they generate (Medina, 2017; Mills, 1997: 18–19). As such, an anti-racist Shakespeare pedagogy demands that instructors center race, racial formation, and racial thinking. It also emphasizes the necessity of understanding race through the presence of non-white racialized Others while underscoring the construction and maintenance of normative white identity. Therefore, an anti-racist Shakespeare pedagogy prohibits the sequestering of conversations about race to the margins of a Shakespeare course, because these ideas are essential to students' lives and they look to their instructors for guidance on how the social, political, and cultural order of the early modern period resonates with their experiences.

Anti-racist Shakespeare pedagogy is an interdisciplinary project that bridges the fields of Shakespeare studies and race studies and requires comprehensive knowledge of these fields to achieve its theoretical and emancipatory aims. The interdisciplinary underpinnings of anti-racist Shakespeare pedagogy facilitate the process by which instructors ground their teaching methods in the roots of racial formation. If their pedagogy is not interdisciplinary, it will not be anti-racist: it will simply be race pedagogy that examines the presence of non-white racialized Others. In "Beauty and the Beast of Whiteness," Kim F. Hall identifies the need for analysis of race in the premodern that is grounded in the work of race studies through the important subfield of whiteness studies. Her argument counters the critical trend locating race in non-white racialized Others, and she cautions that "concentration on the 'other' raises issues of race but may not be anti-racist since it does not necessarily engage issues of power. Such an approach may actually collude in racial inequality" (Hall, 1996: 461). Hall's orientation signals how investigations into the discursive and material production of race must be attuned to how whiteness comes into being and operates as a social force.

Hall indicates how pedagogical inquiry into the representations of race and racial difference can often reproduce the same asymmetrical relations of power that instructors might be attempting to interrogate. On the one hand, non-white racialized Others are more easily legible within Shakespeare and early modern English texts because they are hypervisible against the normative white identity of the authorizing culture. Their somatic difference makes them stand out and apart. On the other hand, by focusing on difference, instructors fall prey to eliding the power that whiteness exerts because whiteness always stands in for the norm of humanity, of culture, and of civilization (Dyer, 2017: 2). In such a formulation, instructors might wittingly or unwittingly reinscribe the centrality of whiteness within their pedagogy. However, as Hall (1996) argues, interdisciplinary, anti-racist praxis can help prevent this outcome because "Renaissance texts provide a wonderful avenue for the study of whiteness" (461).

Readers might be wondering at this point whether we are asking instructors to be race scholars as well as Shakespeare scholars. Indeed, we are. We do not make this proposal lightly; the matter itself is of great importance to us both because of our social locations and our pedagogical and research commitments. Instructors who focus on race for a week or two as one of the topics of their Shakespeare course might be under the impression that they are already doing critical race-work; however, anti-racist Shakespeare pedagogy requires a sustained and critical engagement with issues surrounding race, racism, and racial formation because race does not wait in the lobby of the halls of higher learning. It walks into the room with instructors and with students. It informs every aspect of students' lives, from where and how they sit in their classrooms, to the comfort or discomfort they experience with the course content, to whether they choose to participate in class discussions. Race is a significant part of everyone's social and political location, regardless of whether it is something they think about every day.

The ubiquity of race – that is, its commonplace presence in classrooms and beyond – means that it is always already present. When instructors shy away from critical discussions about race because they fear that such conversations will politicize the classroom, they are making a political choice to ignore the racial realities in front of them. Moreover, when they *do* discuss race, their approach often reproduces the hypervisibility of people of color, rather than interrogating normative, hegemonic, and invisible whiteness. The choice to engage or not engage with race exposes the position of racial privilege, as does the ability to see or not see race: they signal an attachment to "colorblind" racism, which preserves white innocence, and allows people in the dominant group to believe in the meritocratic structure of society and the universality of human experience. Kimberlé Williams Crenshaw, et al. (2019) discusses the "consequences of racial colorblindness as a metaphor for social relations across the academic disciplines," arguing that the university plays an integral role in "constructing, naturalizing, and reproducing racial stratification and domination" through "colorblind" technologies and practices that foment inequity by safeguarding rather than disrupting the race-based foundations of the university (ix). Their critique of institutional "colorblindness" calls for anti-racist teaching practices that are crucial to dismantling the oppressive structures that support white supremacy in education. While we recognize that "colorblind" is an ableist term and do not use it in our own writing, we acknowledge its currency in discourse on diversity, equity, inclusion, and anti-racism. It is reproduced in this Element only when citing the valuable, existing scholarship addressing the harm caused by social and political policies that ignore how race shapes individual and group experiences, particularly those of racially disadvantaged and marginalized people.

Anti-Racist Shakespeare advocates for a theoretical framework grounded in racial literacy and committed to dismantling oppressive structures of power. Such a pedagogy has the potential to fundamentally reorient instructors' approach to course design, informing their choices regarding inclusive and diverse syllabi and assignments. When instructors change how they think about and respond to race in a Shakespeare course, it plants the seed to cultivate the change that anti-racist praxis seeks. The theories we have proposed lay the foundation that helps instructors recognize where they can be more intentional about their anti-racist course design. We follow Felice Blake (2019), who argues that "[i]t isn't enough to include texts by historically aggrieved populations in the curriculum and classroom without producing new approaches to reading" (309). Therefore, we advocate for assigning an array of resources on the anti-racist Shakespeare syllabus, including carefully selected Shakespeare plays that provide students with a range of opportunities to see how race works in his writing; theoretical and scholarly interventions in PCRS, whether as excerpts that accompany the play text or as stand-alone pieces students can examine and discuss fully; and adaptations or reimaginings of his works that trouble Shakespeare's racial politics, suggestions for which we offer at the end of this section. These varied resources help cultivate the new approaches necessary to decode historical and literary cultural production and push back against the dominant white-centric tradition.

Blake's advocacy for developing new reading methods addresses the issue of tokenism that often arises in instructors' attempts to diversify their syllabi. As instructors begin to select secondary sources and scholarship, we recommend they be deliberate about assigning the work of scholars of color in all subfields of Shakespeare studies, not just race. A syllabus that includes broad representation of scholarly identity, particularly in who is considered an authority on Shakespeare, positions scholars from marginalized groups as vital to the field. Without such representation, the implication is that scholars of color do not belong in the discipline, which tacitly communicates to students from under-represented identities that they, too, do not belong. Some may argue that attention to representation could lead to issues of tokenism, which is the inclusion of a limited number of people from marginalized groups to give a false impression of diversity (Ruby, 2020: 675). *Anti-Racist Shakespeare* advocates for a meaningful method of ensuring inclusion that is sensitive to race and identity. The overwhelming whiteness of the field normalizes the idea that Shakespeare is the purview of whiteness by suggesting that the inclusion of scholars of color is tokenistic. When instructors are attentive to who they include on course syllabi, they demonstrate to students the polyphony of scholarly voices in the field and purposefully challenge the stranglehold of whiteness in the discipline.

The broad perspectives that guide an anti-racist Shakespeare course inform the activities that students engage in while in the classroom, giving them a range of ideas that inspire new ways of thinking about the course material. *Anti-Racist Shakespeare*, then, promotes critical thinking that helps students build upon, practice, and apply the varied knowledge that they have acquired. In this way, we conceive of the structure of the course as a process akin to writing a paper, including clarifying the larger vision, and stakes of the course and sequencing readings and assignments to build conceptual frameworks for students over time. This structure is supported by skills-based work, including close reading, interrogating texts, crafting critical arguments, revising writing based on feedback from the course community, and producing a final draft of their emerging ideas. These varying components can help provide a well-rounded approach to engaging with race in Shakespeare's works because they rehearse an iterative process where instructors and students consistently revisit the larger stakes of the course and build upon previous ideas. The steps we have sketched here, which are by no means exhaustive, suggest a course structure that assists students in learning new and difficult concepts through close textual engagement, presents them with opportunities to practice their critical thinking skills in environments where they can make mistakes and be given correction, and leads them to more rigorous analyses and interpretations.

The assignments that emerge from such scaffolding give students an opportunity to showcase their critical thinking on racial formation in Shakespeare with the knowledge that engagement with these matters will be neither seamless nor easy. When instructors create assignments that allow students to process information in a variety of ways, students think more critically about race in their class discussions and writing activities. Discussion questions, free-write prompts, and in-class close reading exercises are excellent ways to have students engage with each other and with the texts in small and large group environments. These assignments can be supported by journal or blog entries where students can practice writing about these topics as well as articulate their personal struggles with the material. We routinely assign weekly reflection responses to specific guiding questions or prompts about our readings because a consistent writing practice in the course often uncovers for instructors and students potential resistance students might have to the course material.

For these reflective writing assignments, instructors may choose to have students submit them privately, so that they are just between the student and the instructor, or publicly, so that other students can read these submissions and respond to their peers. We have successfully tried both approaches and have found benefits and disadvantages in each case that vary based on an instructor's circumstances. A private submission process ensures a confidential space for students who are new to thinking about race and anti-racism where they can make mistakes under the guidance of their instructor. This confidentiality benefits students who might be hesitant to share their responses and resistances to the material for fear that potential errors will be made public. Instructors who are new to anti-racist pedagogy may also prefer private submissions because they can help students process their thinking and their racialized position of power, privilege, or marginalization, without an audience.

What is lost in such a formulation is that the student does not benefit from learning in community with their peers. For that reason, offering an alternative or additional option where students share their ideas publicly can also be a rewarding learning experience. In these instances, students learn from each other, applying the lessons and skills they have gained, and honing those tools through conversation with their peers while still benefiting from their teacher's guidance. These public reflections may still require instructor intervention when students make mistakes; we suggest a public explanation in these moments because this, too, has pedagogical value as students can learn from each other's errors as well as their triumphs. While this suggestion might generate anxiety for instructors, it is imperative that any harmful language or misinformation be immediately corrected in a gentle, supportive, and rigorous way because neglecting to do so will undermine the anti-racist goals of the course. We want to stress that correction must be offered whether the comments are made in private reflections or in public. Without purposeful, constructive, and supportive intervention the damaging comments will circulate with the instructor's silent endorsement.

The protocols we establish for these informal writing assignments also apply to formal writing, to peer review, and to other forms of feedback and peer communication that are central to the work of the course. These practices help students question what they know and further develop their intellectual engagement with the topic. Formal writing assignments similarly allow students to display their learning while facilitating the development of skills in evidence-based argument. Initial formal assignments can be expository, especially when students are exposed to new and unfamiliar theoretical methodologies with complex terminology. Asking them to summarize or explain these texts with a gesture toward application helps students achieve familiarity with critical scholarship and allows instructors to observe the kind of facility students are gaining with the discourse. More advanced writing can focus on the application of the theoretical framework to the primary object of analysis, with critical attention to racial literacy and decoding the racial representations of whiteness and non-whiteness. Regardless of the specific forms these assignments take, an intersectional analysis of race must be central to students' investigations.

Anti-racist pedagogy empowers students to challenge the damaging social hierarchies and power relations that white supremacy fosters and enables. If instructors ignore this dimension in their courses, they risk leaving structural white supremacy in place by simply presenting students with the ability to critique rather than guiding them toward action or intervention in white supremacist systems. Anti-racist Shakespeare pedagogy cannot just be a critique of the invisibility of Shakespearean whiteness and white supremacy in the early modern period: it must also advance a change in the system of racial domination (Kishimoto, 2018). *Anti-Racist Shakespeare* affords instructors and students the possibility to make change, to work toward emancipation from systems of racial power. Without including this vital component of anti-racist pedagogy, instructors risk leaving students disempowered and feeling trapped in a system which they did not create but in which some of them receive material benefits while others are disadvantaged. As Tatum (1992) advises, "exploring strategies to empower students as change agents is thus a necessary part of the process of talking about race and learning about racism" (21). Instructors cannot expose students to the history of centuries-long and ongoing racial domination without offering them an outlet that facilitates change in their attitudes and moves them toward actions that effect transformation if they hope to cultivate an anti-racist pedagogical practice (21).

Building this liberatory framework into course design means offering students alternatives to dominant narratives. We argue that instructors should make space on their syllabi for these counter-hegemonic accounts to expose students to resistant knowledge and artistic practices in Shakespeare. Such practices exhibit methods of engagement that marginalize whiteness and allow other ways of being to emerge. Pairing primary readings with texts from diasporic or Global South artists and writers can illuminate for students the heterogeneous possibilities of depicting, questioning, and repositioning Shakespeare. Reimaginings of Shakespeare by non-white and non-European creatives expose the limits of his white imaginary while also highlighting those qualities in the work that are salient to peoples and cultures beyond the scope of Shakespeare's world-making. Adaptations like Ngugi wa-Thiong'o's *A Grain of Wheat* (1967), which is lightly tethered to *The Tempest*, productions such as the Public Theater's recent performances of the all-Black *Much Ado About Nothing* (2019) and majority actors of color *Richard II* (2020), or Djanet Sears's reimagining of *Othello*, *Harlem Duet* (1997), exposes students to experiences, bodies, and voices of people of color within Shakespeare. These critical engagements with Shakespeare situate the plays in different contexts and challenge the common ways of reading, seeing, and performing them. They allow students to see Shakespeare disrupted or to see "traditional" Shakespeare being performed by actors of color who make their race, ethnicity, and experience a salient part of the performance. These actors are not playing Shakespeare white and therefore seemingly right. Rather they are playing Shakespeare through their identities, thereby resisting the pull of whiteness and reconfiguring what these plays mean. The adaptations of plays that are not usually considered "race plays" introduce new avenues for interpretation and engagement. They offer models for intellectual and creative work in which students can disrupt the normative whiteness of Shakespeare and the world they inhabit.

Teaching Vignette

Shakespeare's Keywords

In this section, we offer a reading of whiteness in Shakespeare's *Henry V* and suggest a close-reading activity we call "Keywords" that can support race-attentive pedagogy. As one of Shakespeare's English history plays, *Henry V* is ideal for investigating the representation and maintenance of whiteness.

The play does not feature any non-white racialized characters, yet it is deeply enmeshed in valorizing an elite and normative form of English masculinity, not only through the war with France, but also through the ethnically heterogenous army that Henry calls upon to wage that war. Most scholars, performers, and readers would agree that *Henry V* is about war and imperial expansion. Its nuanced representation of war simultaneously venerates masculine aggression and honor – realized through the conquest of land and the capture of women – and interrogates the violence that undergirds these endeavors. Nonetheless, warfare facilitates the consolidation of national identity in this play, wherein various forms of ethnic difference that constitute British identity – Scottish, Welsh, and Irish – are subsumed into English through the twin projects of empire and militarism. The multiethnic coalition that Henry assembles to wage his war further results in, we argue, a forging of English whiteness under the banner of masculinity and militarism.

Teaching this play with attention to the different ethnicities represented in Henry's army against the monolithic Other represented by the French, reveals the multiplicity of culture and custom that is contained by the imagined boundaries of the English nation. Henry's multiethnic coalition reveals a fractured nation, one in which English identity must compete with other forms of national identity. His specious war and its attendant themes of masculinity and militarism secure a form of Englishness that can incorporate these internal Others. A critical inquiry rooted in race creates new avenues to explore the important ethnic differences already residing in this play. The play's racial discourse mobilizes "tropes of Blackness" to facilitate a tidy resolution to its fraught ethnic differences (Hall, 1995: 2). Blackness creates and bolsters the whiteness that is central to Henry's image. Attending to race in this play exposes how Englishness transcends its particular ethnic marker to stand in for the nation through its masculinity and militarism, which rely on a shared appeal to whiteness.

In teaching "Keywords," we lay out this argument by guiding our students through the ethnic and class differences in Henry's army and by collective close readings of important passages. Henry's speech before the gates of Harfleur, for example, demonstrates precisely how whiteness is made and framed in the play. We begin this activity by asking students to focus on several key points that are the hallmark of a close reading: the repetition of words and images, the close proximity of ideas and symbols, particularly vivid language, the movement or development of ideas, and the turn or reversal of an argument. We also direct them to look for the language of color and the symbolism that is attached to the use of such language. We are prescriptive in this way because it is helpful in modeling for students our own practice of reading texts for their explicit and implicit meanings.

Henry's speech at Harfleur signals the barbarism inherent in war and invasion. On the surface it is a demand to the town's governor to surrender peacefully or to face the wrath and savagery of Henry's troops, and yet the speech also stands in for Henry's benevolence and virtue, positioning him as a worthy conqueror. We include the monologue below, with italicized keywords, phrases, and images.

> How yet resolves the governor of the town?
> This is the latest parle we will admit;
> Therefore to *our best mercy* give yourselves;
> Or like to *men proud of destruction*
> Defy us to *our worst*: for, as I am a *soldier*,
> A name that in my thoughts becomes *me best*,
> If I begin the *battery* once again,
> I will not leave the half-achieved Harfleur
> Till in her *ashes she lie buried*.
> The gates of *mercy shall be all shut up*,
> And the *flesh'd soldier*, *rough* and *hard of heart*,
> In *liberty of bloody* hand shall range
> With conscience wide as *hell*, mowing like grass
> Your *fresh-fair virgins* and your *flowering infants*.
> What is it then to me, if *impious war*,
> Array'd in *flames* like to the *prince of fiends*,
> Do, with his *smirch'd complexion*, all fell feats
> Enlink'd to *waste and desolation*?
> What is't to me, when *you yourselves are cause*,
> If your *pure maidens fall* into the hand
> Of *hot* and *forcing violation*?

What rein can hold *licentious wickedness*
When down the hill he holds his *fierce* career?
We may as bootless spend our vain command
Upon the *enraged soldiers* in their *spoil*
As send precepts to the leviathan
To come ashore. Therefore, you *men of Harfleur*,
Take *pity* of your town and of your people,
Whiles yet *my soldiers* are in *my command*;
Whiles yet the *cool* and *temperate* wind of *grace*
O'erblows the *filthy and contagious* clouds
Of heady *murder, spoil and villainy*.
If not, why, in a moment look to see
The *blind* and *bloody soldier* with *foul hand*
Defile the locks of your *shrill-shrieking daughters*;
Your *fathers* taken by the silver beards,
And their most reverend heads *dash'd to the walls*,
Your *naked infants spitted upon pikes*,
Whiles the *mad mothers* with their howls confused
Do break the clouds, as did the wives of Jewry
At Herod's *bloody-hunting slaughtermen*.
What say you? will you *yield*, and this *avoid*,
Or, *guilty* in defence, be thus *destroy'd*? (3.3.1–44)

After giving students enough time to work through the text individually or in pairs, we ask a series of guiding questions, starting with what they noticed about the language and the development of the argument in the speech. We then ask what images are critical to supporting the argument and what kinds of reactions such language and symbolism elicit in them. While students will note the language of violence, they often gloss over how that language is enmeshed within a discourse of color. To address this moment of "racial insensitivity," we ask students to close read the passage again; this time we indicate that we are asking them to look for language that signals race, whiteness, and Blackness (Medina, 2017: 249). Specifying the task communicates how racialized language is coded language. We draw their attention to these moments and solicit responses about how and why they are ascribing meaning to certain words. We further ask them to look up words like "besmirched," "complexion," "filthy," "contagious," and "foul," in the Oxford English Dictionary, so that they can understand how their early modern meanings collude with the emerging racial discourse of the period (Adams, 2021). This close reading and keyword activity helps develop racial literacy by asking students to pay attention to race in moments when race seems to be irrelevant. In terms of the speech's relation to the plot, we observe that the conflict here is between the English, who are invaders in this land, and the French, who are defending their homeland. Henry threatens total destruction and degradation if the town does not surrender, and the language of war that he uses is also the language of race.

Henry's suggestion that he and his soldiers might turn to brutal, bloody, and inhumane action relies on the language of besmirching, and defiling – of character, morality, action, and complexion. The comparison is to the "fiend of hell," yet language that symbolically locates savagery and barbarism somatically can easily slip into the language of racial formation. Indeed, Anthony Barthelemy in *Black Face Maligned Race* points out that aligning Blackness with evil has long been a tradition in western Christianity: "whiteness is desired. Blackness is condemned. White is the color of the regenerated, the saved; Black is the color of the damned, the lost" (Barthelemy, 1999: 3). Targeted close reading helps students find and question the mobilization of such color-coded language and consider how this language is implicated in racial formation through its reliance on moral and immoral behavior. The aim of our close reading is not to argue that Henry is Black, but, rather, that language of color is being used in connection to violence to construct inhuman and demonic action. Reliance on such language serves, as Kim F. Hall contends, to instantiate the discourse of race and make certain bodies – those onto whom this color-coded symbolism can easily be mapped – fit for the disciplining that racial discourses like this enact (Hall, 1995: 48). Indeed, the point Shakespeare arrives at through his dependence on color-coded language is Henry's mercy, which is not besmirched or blackened and is therefore, white and pristine.

By accessing the symbolic registers of Blackness, students observe how whiteness gets made and reinforced in this moment to establish Henry's benevolence, which casts onto the fiendish Black Other the threatened violence of the passage. This mercy also extends to Henry's soldiers, symbolically whitening them and their actions. Whiteness as merciful conduct and action secures the fitness of the English to conquer Harfleur and foreshadows their victory at Agincourt. It further corroborates Feagin's contention that the white racial frame encourages a positive orientation toward white people and whiteness (Feagin, 2020: 19). This close reading can be coupled with Henry's St. Crispin's Day speech, where students note the continuity between how fraternity and blood operate to further incorporate members of the disparate ethnicities and classes into the body of the English nation through the monarch's blood, which also serves to whiten them. These examples demonstrate how instructors can talk about race more broadly in the Shakespearean corpus, and how students can put different moments within a play like *Henry V* or across plays in the Shakespeare canon into conversation with each other to identify modes of racial formation. Looking for whiteness helps to destabilize the essentializing of race within people of color, and to mark whiteness as actively being made in the period as a powerful social and cultural subject position, even when people of color are absent from the text.

Teacher Reflection

We end each section by asking teachers to reflect on their pedagogy as it relates to the topic of the section. In this section, we discuss how to create anti-racist Shakespeare courses that disrupt the normative operations of white supremacy in the academy. We centered diversifying authority in course design to counter the overwhelming whiteness of the field. For this "Teacher Reflection" we invite you to consider your goals for an anti-racist Shakespeare course:

- What does cultivating an anti-racist Shakespeare pedagogy mean to you, and how could this perspective inform your approach to course design?
- Consider a course you currently teach: what specific adjustments can you make right now to accomplish your most pressing anti-racist pedagogy goals?

- What specific anti-racist and PCRS methods can you employ to center race in your investigation of assigned texts and through assignments?
- What concerns you about designing an anti-racist course?
- What concerns you about how students will respond to this anti-racist framework?

These reflective questions about anti-racist course design are meant to help teachers examine concerns arising from designing and implementing an anti-racist curriculum. By responding to these questions, whether in solitude or in community with others, in written, oral, or conceptual formats, teachers may feel discomfort with troubling the "traditional" foundations of Shakespeare pedagogy. We hope that creating this reflective space for teachers gives them the opportunity to understand their affective responses more clearly so that they can support their students as they navigate productive modes of discomfort.

3 Building Shakespearean Communities

All of Shakespeare's plays animate questions about community and belonging, particularly who is included or excluded from the dominant society. The central action that motivates Shakespeare's world-making project, therefore, largely depends on the process of preserving old worlds or creating new ones that reaffirm the power regimes of established systems. These plays, thus, make delineations between who does and does not belong – who sustains the system and who might disrupt it – and these lines are largely based on early modern racial formation. In *Henry V*, for example, Henry appeals to brotherhood and blood ties to rally his troops before the battle of Agincourt, including them in the English nation he forges through this war and by claiming them as his kin. In *As You Like It*, Rosalind restores order through an elaborate marriage plot that not only unites her with Orlando and Celia with Oliver, but also the young shepherd Silvius with the obstinate shepherdess, Phoebe, whose misguided desire for Rosalind-as-Ganymede threatens the society Rosalind means to (re)establish. Rosalind categorizes Phoebe's "freestone-colored hand" (4.3.28) and her "Ethiop words, blacker in their effect" (4.3.38) in racializing terms to emphasize the threat of Phoebe's unwitting same-sex and class-inappropriate desire. Like the non-white racialized Others to whom she is compared, Phoebe and her desire for Rosalind-as-Ganymede threatens to contaminate the heterosexual and class-appropriate unions the play authorizes. *Titus Andronicus* similarly foregrounds community and belonging through its investment in the preservation of Roman ideals from outsiders like the Goths as well as from Aaron, the Moor, whose child with Tamora threatens Roman futurity. Shakespeare's plays, therefore, emphasize the preservation of established regimes, question anyone or anything that seem at odds with those existing structures, and seek to destroy that which sits outside of those ideals.

The pervasive themes of community and belonging within Shakespeare's works permeate discussions about inclusion and exclusion in Shakespeare studies. Just as his plays depict the extent to which dominant systems exclude those who seem to threaten the reproduction of existing power structures, similar attachments to long-held, outmoded institutional standards of academic rigor have stunted the growth of scholarship and pedagogy in this area (Erickson & Hall, 2016; Thompson, 2019: 235–36). Though the recent racial reckoning has motivated department heads and educators to diversify the curriculum, many of these changes reproduce the same injustices they seek to dismantle. The reason for this contradictory outcome is diverging interests: despite an institutional aim to be more inclusive, institutions prioritize traditions that are antithetical to anti-racist education. Shakespeare scholarship and pedagogy form one such tradition. Because Shakespeare is integral to the construction and maintenance of whiteness as a structuring mechanism for knowledge production, resistance to reimagining what Shakespeare might mean to a new generation of students and scholars continues to facilitate the structural inequities that frame the academy.

Scholarly and pedagogical innovations from PCRS have addressed questions about belonging in their examination of Shakespeare's works as well as the reception of renewed approaches to Shakespeare in the field. These scholar-teacher-activists model academic rigor in their scholarship and emphasize how reading Shakespeare through the perspectives of historically marginalized groups adds meaning by offering a new epistemological frame. For example, in "Stranger Shakespeare," Ruben Espinosa

(2016) argues that a "Latino/a engagement with Shakespeare would ultimately lead to a more thorough understanding of his cultural capital" (51). By examining the role of the "stranger" in Shakespeare's plays, Espinosa contends that scholars and students can develop a critical vocabulary about belonging that grants insight into who is classified as foreign or familiar in Shakespeare's world. His work is in conversation with scholarship about forms of belonging by Leticia García, Katherine Gillen, Kathryn Vomero Santos, among others. Moreover, this analysis allows for students to reorient their study of Shakespeare through the lens of "outsider" identities that many students might occupy because they cannot lay claim to the whiteness of the dominant culture. Espinosa's extensive work aligns with that of Margo Hendricks and Miles P. Grier in addressing the institutional problems in the field of Shakespeare studies, especially gatekeeping practices that exclude scholars of color. PCRS scholars have built their own communities around their scholarship and identities, including #ShakeRace and #RaceB4Race, but still encounter tremendous backlash in online spaces, exposing the difficulty of community building for scholars of color within traditionally white disciplines. PCRS scholarship and the PCRS community foster belonging and cultivate teaching practices that make community central to the study of Shakespeare.

Because themes of community and belonging are integral to Shakespeare's works, we contend that the classroom can become a laboratory where students think critically about how communities are formed in Shakespeare and beyond. This approach likewise gives students new perspectives in understanding the kind of world they hope to create by examining community and belonging at a distance through a close study of Shakespeare's plays. This section explores the kinds of communal networks that can be cultivated in a classroom setting and reflects on the ways that community building impacts how students understand belonging. In what follows, we reflect on approaches to framing a course as an opportunity to build community and the benefits of such pedagogical practice. In addition, we delineate how to form these communities with compassion and care, how to sustain and enact the vision of the course, how this lens offers a useful foundation for the course, and how these ideas help students read and learn Shakespeare.

The anti-racist approach we advance begins with a central philosophy: that our study of Shakespeare's works is rooted in collaborative thinking generated by a diverse student body. This orientation facilitates community and belonging by emphasizing early modern racial formation, amplifying the stories of forgotten or silenced perspectives, and affirming the value that our most marginalized students bring to discussions about Shakespeare. This process is one of collective action; it is incumbent upon all members of the classroom community to develop their critical thinking and racial literacy as well as to engage with each other from a place of instilling justice in the learning process. Traditional "banking" models of education (Freire, 1970; hooks, 1994) in which instructors lecture to students without an invitation for their intellectual contributions (beyond completion and submission of assigned work) or an examination of perspectives that challenge the status quo perpetuate the unequal power dynamics that an anti-racist course seeks to upend. While a Shakespeare course can never fully escape the structural inequities anti-racism seeks to dismantle – the course is, after all, a component of the institution of education, which will always work to safeguard the academy – we believe that reorienting the power structure of the classroom by cultivating a community-based model of learning will make the inherent problems of these institutional practices apparent to students. These new perspectives prepare students for the examination of course material with an eye toward equity and anti-racism.

Our vision is inspired by thinkers within the humanistic and education fields who have conducted experiential and empirical research on how the development of community bonds between students increases student motivation to activate their own learning potential (De Barros, 2019; Mendoza, 2019; Nieto, 2010). This tendency is especially true when students feel both a sense of belonging *and* detect productive, collaborative movement toward accomplishing a shared goal. In other words, simply creating additional group activities or team projects does not produce the same kind of motivation as classroom environments in which students feel that they are active players in their learning and part of something bigger than themselves (Summers & Svinicki, 2007: 63; Boster, 2019). bell hooks discusses the power of this approach in *Teaching to Transgress*, which advocates for an interactive learning environment that produces pleasure in the learning process. She explains that "[s]eeing the classroom always as a communal place enhances the likelihood of collective effort in creating and sustaining a learning community," and it is in this forum that "[e]xcitement is generated through collective effort" (hooks, 1994: 8). When students know that their presence is an integral component of the class, that their contributions matter, they tend to be motivated to participate more fully.

Prioritizing community, belonging, and enthusiasm in the Shakespeare classroom might generate concern regarding the extent to which this pedagogical practice meets the high academic standards many instructors expect of their students. As bell hooks points out, this approach facilitates a new level of understanding. She states, "I enter the classroom with the assumption that we must build 'community' in order to create a climate of openness and intellectual rigor. Rather than focusing on issues of safety, I think that a feeling of community creates a sense that there is shared commitment and a common good that binds us" (hooks, 1994: 40). hooks reconstitutes rigor through her community-based pedagogical practice. In her estimation, a classroom can be "a democratic setting where everyone feels a responsibility to contribute," which is "a central goal of transformative pedagogy" (39) because students are invested in the outcome of what they co-create. *Anti-Racist Shakespeare* builds upon hooks's philosophy: that a course can achieve high academic rigor through community-based, anti-racist teaching and that this aim is best achieved within an environment of collaboration and co-creation between students and instructors. This orientation to teaching Shakespeare must begin with broadening the scope of the Shakespeare community, which means not only including but especially amplifying the voices of traditionally marginalized scholars, students, and storytellers. Engaging with multi-dimensional approaches to studying Shakespeare trains students to take responsibility for their learning, and how they coexist with others. They acquire a nuanced approach to learning the material, a critical approach to supporting their ideas, and a compassionate approach to communicating their perspectives effectively.

hooks advocates for a method of community-based education that moves away from the concept of "safe spaces" and turns toward a more critically engaged orientation of confronting discomfort in community with others. "Safe spaces" – a concept born out of women's and LGBTQIA+ studies that empowered marginalized individuals in these groups to express their experiences to peers without fear of emotional or physical harm – have been expanded in the context of higher education to include learning spaces where students can opt out of uncomfortable conversations (Flensner & Von der Lippe, 2019). An unintended consequence of this conceptual move is that students who occupy positions of privilege can refuse to participate in conversations about race, racism, and racial formation if they feel uncomfortable with and complicit in the histories of oppression and the systemic reproduction of these injustices (Flensner & Von der Lippe, 2019). Without gaining the historical perspective and racial literacy that comes out of these courses, these students run the risk of upholding violent structures either without their full awareness or with full intention to dismiss anti-racist work. Comfort, as Sara Ahmed (2006) has discussed, "is a feeling that tends not to be consciously felt … Instead, you sink" and settle into what is familiar (154). Discomfort, however, "allows things to move" (154). Through discomfort an individual can "fidget and move around" (154) and, as a result, become aware of any uncertainty they may harbor about a particular topic. Resistance can inhibit their ability to confront something with a new perspective and gain a deeper understanding. For hooks, these stagnant versions of "safe spaces" impede student growth because they restrict students' intellectual and emotional development. Rather than avoid discomfort, hooks suggests that a community-based approach to learning can make the process of sitting with and working through discomfort a productive and enriching learning experience because students undergo the process with the support of their peers and guidance from their instructor.

Our perspective on the community-based model of pedagogical practice as an integral component of anti-racist pedagogy builds on the work of hooks, Ahmed, and others who advocate for addressing discomfort in community. Rather than attempt to create "safe spaces," we advocate for an environment that encourages the growth of each member through sustained community support. While we offer a critique of how "safe spaces" have evolved into zones of privilege, we believe that the classroom should be a space where students can make mistakes, be offered opportunities for correction, and be free of personal attacks based on their identities or their readings of texts. Moreover, we are proposing a classroom community that encourages accountability, dialogue, compassion, and intellectual curiosity coupled with intellectual rigor and productive discomfort.

This classroom orientation lends itself seamlessly to the study of Shakespeare's works. Students not only discover how the plays imagine community and belonging but also how this process facilitates a critical examination of what inclusion and exclusion mean in Shakespeare studies, where they belong in that larger discussion, and how these ideas impact the worlds that they hope to create in their lives. Reconceiving the classroom as a community changes the spirit of how knowledge is produced. While students are often accustomed to an educational environment where information flows unidirectionally from instructor to student, this process reinforces student anxiety about grades and reliance on instructors' opinion of their abilities or sense of worth. Rather than perpetuate this pattern, we advocate for a system of learning that mirrors hooks's (1994) notion of "a democratic setting where everyone feels a responsibility to contribute" (39) and where students and instructors collaborate to build knowledge together. To be clear, we do not suggest that instructors refuse to share their knowledge – which is an amalgam of years of training, learning, and experience. Instead, we are saying that instructors can be more effective as educators when they utilize their expertise, experience, and knowledge to empower their students to discover and to develop their own ideas on their own terms, in their own time, and in the company of peers experiencing the same growth.

Designing a course with a dedication to the empowerment of students creates an equitable learning environment. As any Shakespeare instructor can attest, students enter the Shakespeare classroom – regardless of course level – with assumptions about the author. Because of Shakespeare's cultural capital, students will have been exposed to his works beforehand, whether studying them in previous classes, encountering references in media, watching adaptations, hearing about them from family or friends, or any number of other methods. Students carry ideas into the classroom that Shakespeare and his works hold inherent value. Furthermore, they tend to feel pressure to orient toward Shakespeare's works with the expectation that this value is obvious and transparent. This framework, however, can be alienating, not only for marginalized students who witness characters with shared histories who are vilified, silenced, or erased in his works, but also for students of all backgrounds who may not resonate with his language, his stories, or his perspective. When instructors reinforce a unidirectional flow of knowledge in the Shakespeare classroom, they are likewise enforcing the primacy of Shakespeare. Inviting students to engage in discussions that interrogate the value of Shakespeare and his cultural capital, by contrast, gives students the space to disagree, to dislike, and to disconnect from the weight his works carry, and to deconstruct the formidable structures that perpetuate his position of privilege in the academy.

Reconstituting the classroom as a space of co-creation rather than one of unidirectional knowledge flow builds students' confidence and inspires them to take ownership of their own ideas, as well as invest more in the intellectual and affective work of the course. This transformation occurs because of their agency in creating valuable connections between what they are learning in community with others, allowing them to draw associations between lessons *within* the course, *across* their courses in a given term, and *into* their daily lives – the process by which students find salience with Shakespeare and his works. When students become the guides of their own learning process, the varying skill levels with which they enter the classroom become an added benefit to the learning experience because students can teach each other based on their specific strengths while learning from each other when they require more development. As students learn from each other, the instructor offers context for these emerging ideas by emphasizing content, skills, and techniques. Examining these associations gives students the opportunity to understand their evolutionary process: do these ideas continue to resonate or are they changing over time? Because students experience this process in community, they work together to build a knowledge system that inspires expanded intellectual inquiry and deeper engagement with each other, thus generating a system of support.

Giving students the freedom to be the agents of their own education can generate concerns for instructors about their own role in the classroom. One of the most pressing anxieties that we hear from instructors about developing a community-based model of pedagogy is whether doing so will disempower them and redirect their objectives for the course. We have discovered that this hesitancy often comes from fears about whether they have the capacity to be successful in this process; whether their approach will resonate; whether such an approach compromises student learning; whether they have the time to get through the required material; and so on. This resistance, then, has more to do with confidence, concerns about lack of training and preparation, and an uneasiness about covering required course content, than with a wholesale rejection of the philosophy.

We discuss some of these general apprehensions in more detail at the end of this section, but the concern about authority is integral to how instructors conceptualize their course and requires immediate elaboration. When instructors cultivate an inviting atmosphere in which students can bring their knowledge and observations to the course, disagree with established ideas about a given topic, and shape the course through the expression of their needs and desires, they are ceding authority in a critical way. This adjustment is to be expected, and it yields a more fulfilling learning experience for both instructors and students. As any good teacher will attest, instructors can learn just as much from their students as their students can learn from them. Not only do students' initial encounters with the material create new avenues of exploration for the instructor who has become accustomed to the established ideas associated with the topic, but students' specific views about the material can also bring new insight into the field. A community-based model of pedagogical practice renegotiates how information moves in a course. Far from threatening instructors' positions as experts, this approach invites innovative orientations to familiar material. It likewise repositions instructors as guides rather than the sole source of knowledge, simultaneously acknowledging instructors' experience even as students direct their learning process by expressing their needs, queries, and curiosities.

The process of creating this collaborative environment begins with establishing a set of guidelines written collectively by students and instructors that sets the tone for the emerging classroom community. We call these co-created guidelines, goals, and policies Community Norms. These agreements help shape the classroom dynamic and give students and instructors a clear vision for how the course might unfold. They highlight the values that the students prioritize and give instructors a better idea of the kind of learning environment students need to thrive in the course. Community Norms also give students an understanding of what is expected of them, by their peers and by their instructor. The process by which these Community Norms are established, which we offer later in this section, permits potential gray areas in pedagogy to emerge: because students express their needs, the motivation behind those needs also emerges, giving the class an opportunity to understand why a particular value is important. This context confirms the policy's importance, which encourages all community members to respect the guidelines as they develop. We use Community Norms to name the mutual agreements that we co-create with students to emphasize the communal conventions that we establish in our classrooms. Other terms for this practice might be Community Agreements, Contracts, Standards, or Measures. As Brian Arao and Kristi Clemens (2013) demonstrate, creating such "ground rules" and paying attention to naming practices can manifest a learning space where social justice activities can be "actualized" (142). This roadmap allows for generative conversations as the course progresses because students are already aware of the possible directions conversations could go and what kinds of allowances they are permitted as they explore.

Community Norms should be a living document that takes new shape as the course progresses. They are most effective when established early in the term but can be revised as needed. Not only does establishing Community Norms set a tone for collaborative learning in the course, but also it signals to students that their contributions are necessary in building worlds – within and beyond the classroom. Students feel empowered, motivated, and eager to learn with and from the community because they shaped it. Therefore, by establishing Community Norms, students experience a series of important values from the outset of the course, including the feeling of empowerment, the understanding of what is expected of them, the feeling of responsibility to the group, deeper engagement with the work of the course, preparedness for possible directions the course might take, and accountability toward self and others in maintaining the learning environment that the group has envisioned. As a result, students feel more invested in the success of the course and are more likely to hold themselves and each other accountable.

Even as Community Norms are important in setting a strong foundation for an anti-racist classroom, they do not guarantee that problems will not arise. Rather they ensure that when things do go wrong, there is a roadmap that everyone can turn to for guidance on how best to proceed. When a student strays from the intention of the document, their classmates and instructor can intervene to bring everyone back into alignment, through gentle reminders, powerful questioning, guiding, and critical analysis. It is possible that some students will act in bad faith, though these moments tend to be rare when the course is set up with accountability as a core value. Because each student is a contributor to the Community Norms, the instructor can intervene by reminding the student of their agreement toward the protocol they helped to create. By turning to this document, the instructor can invite dialogue rather than exert unilateral authority – i.e. asking the student why they broke a policy they helped to create rather than deducting points or shutting them down – which increases the odds that the student will choose to continue to be part of the community rather than disconnecting and maintaining an antagonistic approach to the work of the course.

The ongoing process of crafting Community Norms as a living document that evolves with the class ensures that it remains relevant to the work of the course. The Community Norms agreement should always remain accessible to the community; therefore, we recommend housing it online in the course's learning management system. We recommend revisiting Community Norms regularly, more frequently at the start of the course to emphasize the shared commitments of the community and then as the need arises. The process of crafting and returning to Community Norms is crucial when considering the potential to center anti-racism and social justice in the course. Community Norms can easily become performative, where each student states a generalized idea or cliché that loses meaning with each iteration. Rather than simply transpose these ideas onto the document and move onto the next suggestion, we recommend that instructors take the opportunity to examine critically the proposed policy with students. This intervention may include rearticulating the suggestion to ensure full comprehension, asking guiding questions that might invite more clarity or precision, and opening the forum to invite other students to help add dimension and purpose to the idea. An example might be, if a student suggests a Community Norm that states "We should respect everyone's opinion," the instructor might ask for more clarification by asking guiding questions like, What does it mean or look like to "respect" everyone's opinion? What if the opinion is harmful to a person or group of people? Should the course favor *opinions* about the material or themes rather than textual engagement, critical analysis, and historical context? How might we revise this well-intentioned norm so that it is more specific about the kind of course we hope to create? Focusing on dialogue gives instructors the opportunity to infuse the document with anti-racist considerations. By challenging the students to assess whose ideas are shared, when, and why, instructors can help them perceive larger structures more clearly.

When engaging in this process with students, we find it helpful to begin with a modeling exercise. First, we recommend that instructors suggest the initial Community Norm as an example, such as, "What is said here, stays here; what is learned here, leaves here." Next, offer context and an explanation:

> Because we will discuss some challenging topics, we want everyone to feel encouraged as they learn how to articulate their ideas about this new subject matter. Therefore, we want to refrain from disclosing what was said and by whom outside of our class community. However, we will be learning valuable skills about how to discuss these topics as well as learning more about these topics in depth; we want to encourage each other to take these lessons into our daily lives.

Finally, instructors should invite students to offer suggestions or feedback on their proposed Community Norm. This exchange often leads to deeper exploration of the existing idea or introduces new ideas that can become part of the document. When instructors model the process for students, they learn how to proceed and replicate the process with each other. In addition, the process allows instructors to guide the discussion as well as to contribute to the document in equal measure. Instructors are also members of the course community. This collaborative, community-building exercise permits instructors to execute their vision while enfolding their students' needs into the foundation of the course through powerful communication. Some possible and common Community Norms include:

- critique the idea, not the person
- be open to critique; we are all learning
- give each other the benefit of the doubt
- allow each other a second or third chance to express a point
- we assume good intentions; we take responsibility for impact

When instructors consider implementing Community Norms, they often express a series of concerns. Some common considerations may include fears about losing authority, negotiating disagreements between students during the Community Norms activity, or navigating recommendations that instructors would prefer to reject. If jumping into this practice is challenging, we recommend starting slowly rather than foregoing the practice. For example, instructors can implement Community Norms for a particular assignment or a specific component of the class as a small-scale intervention. Below, we have enumerated several of the most common "what if" scenarios and our responses:

But what if . . .

1. . . . my students can't agree on a particular guideline?

> → It is a rare occasion when students fundamentally disagree about a particular Community Norm, but instructors can reframe possible stumbling blocks as learning opportunities to empower everyone. When students do not agree on a recommendation, it is best to address the source of the disagreement immediately by

asking guiding questions. Instructors might rearticulate
the two stances and the reasons for those stances to the
whole class, and then invite the class to brainstorm ways
to reconcile them. These moments – though rare – are
exceptionally powerful, especially at the start of the term
because they build trust: students see, in real time, that
they can work together to find a resolution, and they see
that the instructor is there to support their exploration.

2. ... I don't agree with my students?

> → There may be an occasion when students will offer
> a Community Norm that diverges from instructors' origi-
> nal vision of the course. In some cases, this suggestion
> could be productive, and instructors might want to con-
> sider allowing it. In other cases, it would be pertinent for
> instructors to provide a revision of the Community Norm
> to explain why it may not be appropriate for the course
> (e.g. if it contradicts other policies the students have
> already agreed upon or conflicts with university expecta-
> tions). To ensure the most fluid process that anticipates
> this possibility, we recommend that instructors clarify for
> themselves what their limitations are in advance.

3. ... some students would prefer to get direction from me?

> → Some students feel discomfort with Community
> Norms simply because it is different from what they are
> accustomed to, which is to rely predominantly on
> instructor feedback, framework, and guidance to pro-
> gress and improve. However, we believe that challenging
> these students to be agents in knowledge production has
> tremendous pedagogical payoff. Students want to learn
> and grow; depending too heavily on a teacher's guidance
> can inhibit this growth. Participating in the development

of Community Norms offers students an opportunity to
practice the necessary leadership to work with others and
to take responsibility.

4. ... it compromises my authority in the classroom?

→ We contend that perpetuating the teacher-student
power dynamic does not guarantee authority or leadership in a course. Rather, we argue that the best form of
leadership comes when instructors model for students
how to take ownership over their ideas and their roles
in a community. Therefore, Community Norms reorient
power by putting it into a different context and empowering students to learn how to be effective leaders. The
impact of the activity is in students' ability and opportunity to articulate their needs and to have those needs met
by peers and the instructor. Sharing power exhibits the
authority of the instructor rather than compromises it.

5. ... my vision of the course gets lost by conceding to their
preferences?

→ Instructors are also part of the course community and
their preferences are just as important as the students'.
Developing Community Norms is a process by which
instructors and students engage in conversation to
express what the course will look like together.

Anti-racist pedagogy requires discussing difficult and sensitive subjects.
One way to mitigate the uneasiness that can permeate the classroom is
through the development of Community Norms. They create a democratic
space for dialogue and for student investment in the work of the course.
They can significantly reduce potential problems because of the roadmap
collectively created to navigate the challenging but rewarding terrain of
anti-racist pedagogy.

Teaching Vignette

Inside/Outside with *Titus Andronicus*

Titus Andronicus, as a play concerned with the incorporation of the Other into the imperial body of the dominant culture, is perfectly positioned to draw out questions of community in the classroom through a meaningful discussion about empire, and about who can and cannot be incorporated into the imperial, political, and cultural body. The foundation of *Titus Andronicus*, therefore, brings notions of community to bear – particularly with regard to who is classified as *inside* the dominant society, and therefore belongs, and who is *outside* the dominant society, and therefore is a potential threat. This orientation toward the play is a useful basis for what we call the "Inside/Outside" activity, which deepens students' questioning and under-standing of how individuals are categorized, the value assigned to these categorizations, and how this process affects the larger community dynamic. What we propose can be adapted to meet the needs of the course, whether it is presented as an in-class activity, an assignment that is devel-oped over time, or even expanded into a final project asking students to put ideas of community, belonging, and exclusion into conversation with other plays on the syllabus.

The basis of the "Inside/Outside" activity is to guide students through an examination of the characters in the play, where students identify the char-acteristics, origins, physical appearance, speech patterns, and actions of the characters to determine whether they are considered "inside" or "outside" the dominant society and to investigate who gets to make this determination. We recognize that binary methods of classification, such as "Inside/Outside," can be limiting; therefore, the activity should account for how certain characters inhabit multiple classifications or problematize the inside/outside binary itself. "Inside/Outside" likewise invites students to begin asking more nuanced questions about belonging by posing questions such as:

- What is the significance of an empire that welcomes outsiders into its realm?
- How might the categorization of someone as an outsider impact if and how they are incorporated into the dominant society?

- Is assimilation the only way for this incorporation to occur?
- What somatic factors make assimilation im/possible?
- What are the criteria that are considered (and by whom) to determine whether the outsider is a (physical or ideological) threat to the dominant society?

Students make their determinations based on the details they excavate from the text through close reading practices; these details offer clues that support their interpretations and provide a basis for why such a categorization exists within the society of the play. Students' assessments can then be translated into the broader context of community, further developing their analytical skills as they engage with the primary material and with their own broader social context.

In their study of *Titus Andronicus*, students note significant details about the characters and their classifications. They may observe, for example, that the Roman characters are associated with nobility and rule, a contrast to the signifiers describing the captives Titus has brought to Rome from his successful war with the "barbarous" Goths (1.1.34). Problematizing the common ways that students might understand race as Blackness, Tamora's "hue" (1.1.263), which Saturninus twice refers to as "fair" (1.1.265; 340), draws attention to her skin color. In her foundational reading of this scene, Francesca T. Royster interprets Tamora racial classification as "extreme," "distanc[ing] [her] from the more moderate Romans" (Royster, 2000: 439). Students also notice that the stage directions accompanying Aaron's entrance describe him as "a Moor" (1.1), which is significant because students have been trained to see race in non-whiteness. Aaron's silent presence onstage for the entirety of the first scene renders him a visual spectacle, his skin conveying meaning to the audience even as his presence accentuates the hyper-whiteness of the Goths. The "Inside/Outside" activity encourages students to think about both the phenotypic expressions and the assumed behaviors associated with the characters as the play progresses. In other words, it asks them to think about race as whiteness and non-whiteness; as Roman and non-Roman. Because of the moral degeneracy associated with figures like Tamora, Aaron, Chiron, and Demetrius within the play, the terminology that describes these characters accrues more meaning over time – there is a direct correlation between the hyper-whiteness of the Goths and the Blackness of "the Moor" and their growing barbarousness with each violent act they plot and undertake.

The vision of empire that *Titus Andronicus* offers unearths anxieties about what that future empire might look like, and the kinds of threats that might destabilize the actualization of this desire for expansion. While the play narrates Roman history, it also harnesses England's own Roman inheritance and activates England's nascent imperial fantasies. Because the English see themselves as heirs to Rome's imperial legacy, *Titus Andronicus* offers a proxy site through which to experiment with English community formation. As Royster (2000) argues, the play is most troubled by the threat that lies *within* a society. This danger is crystallized in the mixed-raced body of not only Tamora and Aaron's child, described in the stage directions as "a blackamoor Child" and called "a devil" (4.2.64) by Tamora's nurse, but also in the "fair" (4.2.155) infant of a Moor, Muliteus, and his (white) Roman wife. To save his child, Aaron offers to replace his baby with the other – fair – newborn, charging Chiron and Demetrius with bribing the new mother with gold and the promise of a prosperous future for her child as the emperor's heir. Aaron, meanwhile, plans to live with his Black baby in the wild. Royster's reading of this scene uncovers how Aaron's scheme simultaneously opens the door for Aaron's child to return to Rome as a conqueror and for white-passing mixed-race babies to grow up as future Roman emperors, undetected by the Roman state. These potential internal threats to a pure, white, civilized Rome are rooted in anxieties of racial Otherness.

The "Inside/Outside" activity offers students the opportunity to explore the imperial and racial contours of community formation. After students have carefully examined and questioned what the play's characters and their respective geographies signify, they are better equipped to read the social location and bodies of the mixed-race children that appear at the end of the play. These children pose an internal threat that haunts the idea of empire, and the ambiguity of their fates suggests an ongoing fear about whether the Roman empire – or the possibility of an English one – could ever yield the pure, white future that was promised. *Titus Andronicus* tries to answer this fear with the presence of young Lucius: a hopeful future contained in the body of a young, white, Roman who can continue the imperial project. Despite the play's attempt to restore Rome's future, it ends with the promised and accomplished deaths of Aaron and Tamora, a rhetorical union that reanimates the memory of the threat from within. The play simultaneously raises and negates the possibility of racial purity within the imperial fantasy it depicts. Empire requires contact with difference through various modes of conquest, both martial and marital. While incorporating Others into the self might seem a function of empire, it also instantiates the fear of cultural and racial mixture and miscegenation. Attending to whiteness in *Titus Andronicus* reveals how these anxieties and fears are managed in order to facilitate the illusion of a racially pure empire.

The anxieties about empire formation and the threat of the Other that guide *Titus Andronicus* are a productive starting point for students to deepen the lessons they will have begun about community from the outset of the course. If their Community Norms activity initiates affective responses with regard to questions of belonging – particularly in the process of outlining what that might look like within the context of the classroom – then these responses might evoke larger questions about who belongs, in what contexts, and according to whose desires. Some questions might include:

- Why are these micro-level policy engagements so difficult to actualize on a macro-level?
- What are the structural issues that facilitate the categorization of individuals, whether they fundamentally align with the dominant mission of a society or not?
- How can individuals become enfolded within that society if such assimilation is even possible?
- What other methods of world-making might exist?

Students' orientation toward the play initiates complex questions of belonging that inform their readings of *Titus Andronicus*, and helps them to see the structural mechanisms in place that ultimately categorize and assign value to human beings, whether that is to assume inherent value for anyone inside the system or to deny value to anyone who is seen as outside of the system.

Teacher Reflection

We end each section by asking teachers to reflect on their pedagogy as it relates to the topic of the section. In this section, we demonstrate how co-creating community in the classroom helps cultivate an anti-racist pedagogy. We argued that establishing Community Norms as a classroom community centers inclusion and belonging, encourages students' personal and intellectual growth, and empowers them to be agents in their education. For this "Teacher Reflection," we invite you to consider the community you envision for the courses you teach:

- What does a classroom community mean to you?
- How can you establish a community-based foundation for your course?
- What are your non-negotiable course policies, and why are these values important to you?
- To what extent are you willing to adapt your teaching toward your students' needs and preferences?
- What are you willing to do to support your students as they work through these ideas in community and under your guidance?

These reflective questions about building a transformative classroom community are meant to help teachers consider how instilling their students with a sense of belonging helps to combat racism. By responding to these questions, whether in solitude or in community with others, in written, oral, or conceptual formats, teachers may feel discomfort when confronting the systemic exclusion of individuals and groups. We hope that creating this reflective space for teachers inspires them to cultivate inclusive and anti-racist practices that empower them and their students.

4 The Salience of Shakespeare

As *Anti-Racist Shakespeare* uncovers, Shakespeare's whiteness bolsters his elite cultural capital because his racial invisibility animates his position of universality. We counter the universality myth through our concept of salience, which emerges when interlocutors, instructors, students, readers, audiences, and performers of Shakespeare develop a racial literacy framework. Our concept of salience deviates from the technique of emphasizing Shakespeare's relevance, a common practice in the Shakespearean classroom. Relevance assumes that students can understand Shakespeare through his universality, making Shakespeare the author of their experiences. However, salience centers students' orientation and affective connection toward what strikes them as vital in the work based on what "leaps" off the page (*OED*, salient, adj. and n.), which we argue is an active response to reading Shakespeare that animates students' investments in ideas and themes that emerge from his work. Salience prioritizes student agency over Shakespearean authority and points to how Shakespeare can serve students' intellectual growth.

In this section, we examine three different modes of salience, identifying various modalities in which Shakespeare's racial salience can emerge. Coupled with racial literacy, salience targets specific parts of the Shakespearean canon that prompt affective, intellectual, and artistic responses in students because they speak to aspects of their experiences, interests, identities, or social locations. Racial literacy is a key component of salience because it helps students critically analyze how identity can be crucial to the process of attachment to literary texts and characters, helping them unpack the unacknowledged normativity of the dominant culture in constructions of universalism. The first mode of salience advocates for student performance as a way to encourage them to think about their physical bodies and affective responses in relation to the Shakespearean text. Performance exposes how the body is an interpretive tool to understand and analyze Shakespeare and challenge the hegemony of whiteness. This orientation provides new information to students about Shakespeare that affects how they encounter him and his works long after the class ends. In the second mode of salience, we highlight how the lack of racial literacy in mainstream media contributes to forms of embodiment in Shakespeare that are exclusionary, revealing that the myth of Shakespeare's universality is what these creators find salient and seek to reproduce. The third mode of salience attends to a counter-narrative to these mainstream media interpretations, such as race-attentive adaptations that question and challenge Shakespeare's powerful position and disrupt the stranglehold he has on literature, theater, and culture. These different modes of salience demonstrate how Shakespeare's dominance can be challenged through embodiment and performance that limit his ability to speak for humanity and have the last word on race.

Performance can be an important method through which students can reinforce and support Shakespeare's salience to their lived experiences. Shakespeare's plays are performance scripts that mandate engagement through embodiment. When instructors shift students' orientation toward these objects by building performance into their courses with attention to students' identities, they will find that students begin to reevaluate their relation to Shakespeare's works. Recognizing that instructors teach in differently resourced programs or departments, *Anti-Racist Shakespeare* proposes performance strategies that can be incorporated into most, if not all, classrooms. We advocate for performance-based teaching because it requires students to actively participate in the process of making meaning in Shakespeare through their bodies as well as their minds. Moreover, this perspectival shift can often introduce new hermeneutical avenues for students so that they begin to think about the plays differently. Performance feeds into textual analysis, just as textual analysis feeds into performance. Most importantly, performance exposes the white racial invisibility of Shakespeare's works because it is an embodied experience where students bring their identities into their roles.

The ubiquity of Shakespeare's universality suggests that anyone can seamlessly step into Shakespeare's characters. Indeed, universality promises actors that in performing Shakespeare, their identities recede into the background thus allowing the role to take center stage. However, societal structures are governed by racial regimes and race operates through a visual register, which means that it makes itself known through the body in a process Frantz Fanon (1988: 22) identifies as the epidermalization of race. If performing Shakespeare erases the body of the actor and layers onto that body the unraced Shakespearean character, then the performance actively whitewashes the actor's physical being. It shrouds the actor in the normative, white identity latently signaled in Shakespeare's canon. While Shakespeare's texts are notorious for their lack of specificity about characters and their racial markings (except for a select few), the common assumption is that these characters are white, and consequently, racially invisible. Neither actors of color nor students of color are racially invisible: their non-white racialized bodies are texts to be read in a white supremacist society (Hall, 2021a: 133). Erasing race and its significance in students' lives from their performances of Shakespeare through such race-neutral and whitewashed methods attests to the power of whiteness to regulate and control. Instead, a color-conscious approach to performance (Akhimie, 2020) that attends to identity and allows identity to inform the construction of character helps students make Shakespeare work for them (salience), rather than transforming themselves to fit into Shakespeare (relevance).

Bringing performance into Shakespeare courses that are focused on literary analysis can appear daunting. We offer some strategies to incorporate performance in small- and large-scale ways to encourage the use of performance as a challenge to the normative identities in Shakespeare. The simplest way to add a performance component into the course is to ask students to read scenes together, out loud. This approach, while still tethered to the text, gives students a chance to hear Shakespeare in each other's voices, in different cadences and accents. Building upon this activity, instructors can ask students to pick a monologue, review and mark up the text to identify key beats and words they think should be emphasized, and listen to each other's varied interpretations of the same scene. Alternatively, students can record themselves reciting that monologue multiple times, where every recording highlights a different aspect of the speech that introduces a new dimension or concern of the monologue that the student wants to emphasize. Students should not worry about maintaining meter in their recitation, nor should they be overly concerned about correct pronunciation. In fact, if some constructions in the passage seem overly archaic, students should be encouraged to edit them, to make them fit the meaning students want to convey. While such revisions might seem objectionable to textual purists, we want to stress that all modes of Shakespeare performances make editing choices to support their vision, and so this exercise invites students into that creative process while also empowering them to assemble and disassemble Shakespeare's words.

More collaborative performance options can be productive for courses that can support extended projects. The tableau is one technique that offers a silent, visual, and embodied representation of a scene. The tableau helps students picture Shakespeare's words in action and see the relations between characters by where and how they are located on the stage. For this assignment, instructors can give students a whole scene or a section of a scene and ask them to arrange themselves in pairs or groups so that the relationship between characters and the power dynamics of the scene are communicated through each character's location on stage. Once students have designed their tableau, they perform it for the class, and the class evaluates it based on how clearly the tableau has communicated what happens in the scene. These exercises introduce students to performance, helping them get comfortable moving around the classroom and interacting with each other in a new way. These embodiment activities can also be utilized with Shakespeare's narrative poems and sonnets, especially because they also are telling stories.

More advanced performances can be built upon these techniques after students have become familiar with embodiment as a pedagogical practice and gained a deep understanding of the literature itself. Through these activities, students can begin to address the question that Carol Mejia LaPerle (2022) asks in her introduction to *Race and Affect in Early Modern English Literature*, "how does race feel?" Such performances, whether they focus on one scene, a selection of scenes, or the entire play, should attend to identity and the various structures of marginalization in the play. This focus emphasizes that the pedagogical goal of the performance is to advance an argument about the play's racial dynamic through the process of embodiment. In other words, the performance is communicating something to its audience. Within that process of communication, students will want to consider how their identities are being depicted and how their own social location informs the character they play (Dadabhoy, 2020b: 232). Instructors can invite them to reflect upon how they can lean into or out of their identity, and what is gained and lost in the message they want to deliver through those choices. Students should be encouraged to play with Shakespeare's text in their performances, such as attending to character development, setting, costuming, music, and so on, so that they emphasize the elements that are salient to them, whether on the grounds of identity or other aspects of their lived experiences. Finally, their performance should have an argument or make a claim that informs their choices, which become apparent through the performance decisions they make. Advancing a thesis through performance makes explicit for students the connections between the "usual" work of literary studies and the embodiment of Shakespeare. It also helps them articulate their goals in crafting a performance that is racially literate, inclusive, and that adapts Shakespeare to suit their purposes.

When students perform and embody Shakespeare's scripts by exploring what they find salient with attention to identity and race, it prepares them to analyze the racial underpinnings of other Shakespearean performances, adaptations, and apparitions, by which we mean the way Shakespeare haunts popular culture. Instructors can assign such depictions on their syllabi to show students how the tools of racial literacy as well as their work on embodiment and performance can help them decipher racial coding in other domains. Pop culture's mobilizations of Shakespeare often rely on his cultural capital with appeal to his relevance to their contemporary moment. Shakespeare becomes, in such deployments, the cultural inheritance of whiteness. Pop culture adaptations harness the Shakespearean inheritance by highlighting how his plots can find tidy analogues to the follies and foibles of contemporary life.

Both inheritance and legacy are key themes explored and exploited in the television show *Succession*, whose title puns on inheritance and the right to rule; thus, the Shakespeare references are unavoidable. A modern-day *King Lear*, *Succession* follows the billionaire Roy family, and their multi-media business at a time when the company is potentially shifting power away from the ailing patriarch and into the hands of his opportunistic children. After its first two seasons, the show received criticism for its predominantly white cast. Though its third season attempted to answer these critiques, specifically with the addition of the character Lisa Arthur, a Black woman and attorney, the show has been unapologetic about its majority white narrative (Newman-Bremang, 2021). In a 2020 interview, show creator Jesse Armstrong fell back on the excuse of "realism," arguing that "[o]ur show is about a white family of billionaires, media moguls" and claiming it "would not be reflecting reality if we made our central world more diverse than the higher echelons of corporate America are" (Aceshowbiz, 2020). Even when the show *does* diversify its cast, as critics have noted, it does not demonstrate a full understanding of the racial dimensions that characters of color bring with them (Holloway, 2021; Newman-Bremang, 2021). These characters become pawns for the Roy family *and* the show, offering little room for critique about the society the show attempts to represent "realistically."

Succession's failure in racial literacy and its missed opportunity to engage critically with race obscure the whiteness that enables the family's high-stakes shenanigans and animates the daily deceptions that often occur at the expense of people of color. Armstrong, in another interview, specified that his characters were interesting because they were "not unwatchable" and resembled "someone you know in real life" (Wise, 2021). The idea of "someone you know in real life," however, depends on the communities and identities familiar to the audience; therefore, Armstrong gestures toward whiteness without acknowledging its centrality to the community of *Succession*. Through the unfolding of *Succession*'s plot, audiences – by Armstrong's account – become more sympathetic to the characters in a system that uses people of color to advance their own objectives and who benefit from white supremacy. *Succession* seems uninterested and is ill-equipped to engage in any significant discussions about race because its creators are either oblivious to or disinterested in how whiteness works to advance itself as an unraced position of power and privilege. By resorting to the idea of "realism" to limit characters of color on the show so that only white people hold power and privilege, the creators illustrate their own investment in white supremacy. Moreover, Shakespeare's presence as the author whose work largely underwrites *Succession* further points to the overwhelming epistemic whiteness that subtends the show and the basis for its investment in reproducing these racist narratives. Despite his much-touted universality, Shakespeare's characters, like the characters in *Succession*, are overwhelmingly white, and his plots occasionally include token characters of color meant to advance the predominant whiteness of his plays. Thus, adaptations like *Succession* can dismiss the charge of racial homogeneity by pointing to the source material's invisible racial character, especially when the source has been historically categorized as universal.

Because our students have developed their racial literacy skills through embodiment exercises, they are well-positioned to identify the limitations of shows like *Succession*. One way to incorporate a multi-season show that offers extensive fodder for discussion in the classroom is to assign clusters of resources that include scenes from the show and paratextual readings like the articles about the show that we have discussed. Instructors can prompt students by asking how identity is embodied in the characters on screen, through their appearance, actions, voice, and motivations. Such guided inquiry invites students to apply lessons from their performance exercises, using visual, auditory, and textual evidence to support their observations. When students rely on what they find salient vis-a-vis the Shakespearean canon and its reimaginings or apparitions, they are better equipped to analyze and engage with cultural artifacts like *Succession*. Their critical investigations of such works, inflected by their own salient and racially literate interpretations, render them astute readers of the supposed universality of whiteness on display in these productions and they cease to be uncritical consumers of normative and hegemonic white supremacy.

Not all Shakespearean afterlives have such investments in whiteness; indeed, the race-attentive Shakespearean adaptations that inform our third mode of salience offer a counterpoint to those commitments. This mode centers on adaptations and reimaginings of Shakespeare that offer counter-narratives, or disruptions, to Shakespeare's vision (Erickson, 2013; Mehdizadeh, in press), and intervenes in a larger discussion in adaptation studies with regard to fidelity. The lingering question that emerges time and again where adaptation is concerned is whether a particular reimagining *counts* as an adaptation, the judgment for which largely rests on its ability to faithfully reproduce Shakespeare. However, as Joyce Green MacDonald, L. Monique Pittman, Margaret Jane Kidnie, and Vanessa Corredera, among others have argued, such criticisms rely on the fantasy of Shakespeare's assumed authority and the white supremacist structures upon which he builds worlds. In her reading of Tim Blake Nelson's *O* (2001), an adaptation of *Othello* set in high school and starring Mekhi Phifer (Odin) and Julia Stiles (Desi), Corredera (2017) argues that both the film and criticism of it offer a white "recuperative reading" of race, particularly in the play's relocation to the American South. As she states, "Odin's representation as a young black man who wreaks havoc on a prep school in the Deep South taps into pernicious American stereotypes about black masculinity." She further demonstrates that "the film trades in and ultimately reifies malignant American fantasies – both historical and modern – about black men that overwhelm the film's attempts at positive representation." Nelson's *O* misses an opportunity to provide a counter-narrative that might bring Shakespeare's harmful race-making to the surface, or to bring to the forefront the ways in which whiteness structures the play, instead duplicating the play's inherent racism. Corredera's race-attentive reading models an interpretive practice for students that disrupts the white supremacist framework informing *O*'s problematic engagement with race and emphasizes that not all adaptations can challenge the racism that animates *Othello*. In determining how to guide students through these adaptations, we suggest selecting ones that either subvert the race-logics of white supremacy or showcase these race-logics, as long as they are accompanied by scholarship like Corredera's so that students can witness models of intervention in Shakespeare's racial politics (Mehdizadeh, in press).

Anti-Racist Shakespeare returns to *Othello* and its afterlives here because its adaptations offer a rich archive through which to think about race as whiteness and Blackness. These adaptations, which are also artistic interventions by Afro-diasporic creators, are exemplary for anti-racist pedagogy because they engage with white racial dominance, which relies on Black racial subordination, and they reclaim Black agency within that framework. In short, they powerfully deny Shakespeare the last word on Blackness and on humanity. Djanet Sears's *Harlem Duet* (1997) is a reimagining of Shakespeare's *Othello* that centers the perspective of the sybil who "[i]n her prophetic fury sew'd the work" (3.4.84) of the fated handkerchief. Sears's play follows three iterations of the same couple – HIM and HER in the Civil War era, HE and SHE in the Harlem Renaissance, and Othello and Billie in the present – to meditate on the continuous repetition of racial injustice over time (Mehdizadeh, 2020: 14). In each timeline, Othello leaves Billie – whose name is short for Sybil – for a white woman named Mona, leading audiences anachronistically into the seventeenth-century setting of *Othello*.

Sears's adaptation is an example of a disruptive adaptation and of racial salience: it is a rumination on Shakespeare, race, gender, and the theater that addresses guiding questions Sears has asked of herself as a Black woman and playwright. In an interview with Mat Buntin for the Canadian Adaptations of Shakespeare Project, Sears, (2004) recounts these questions: "How could I begin to look at *Othello* from my own perspective? What do I think of him? Who would he be if he were alive today? What kind of mythic archetype has he become?" Like the questions we pose to our students when we offer them salience as a method for engaging with Shakespeare's texts, the questions Sears asked to herself reflect her social location as well as that of Shakespeare's in relation to how his work has structured Black identity. Her answers come through *Harlem Duet*, which recovers the sybil from the margins of *Othello* by considering who Othello is and what he represents through the eyes of this mystical, magical, and mysterious Black woman. Sears's technique is reminiscent of Twine's (2010) racial literacy framework: she adopts an intersectional approach to identifying racism – in Shakespeare and in the theater as an institution – and harnesses "an analytical orientation and a set of practices that reflect shifts in perceptions of race, racism and whiteness. It is a way of perceiving and responding to racism that generates a repertoire of discursive and material practices" (8). When instructors assign texts like *Harlem Duet* they can deepen students' developing racial literacy practices. Sears models salience through her engagement with Shakespeare and creates something new out of his cultural capital.

One way *Harlem Duet* engages with racial literacy is to interrogate knowledge production as a racializing regime. It questions the power that canonical authors wield when they write about race, a power that allows their claims to circulate as truth. In Act 1 scene 4, Billie hears a knock at the door. Othello has returned to the apartment that he and Billie once shared on the corner of Martin Luther King and Malcolm X Boulevards to gather the remainder of his belongings before beginning his life with Mona. Othello and Billie begin sifting through the books on the bookshelves in a moment that offers revealing commentary on the production of knowledge. Othello reads the titles: *African Mythology*, *The Great Chain of Being*, *Black Psychology*. His questions "[M]ine or yours?" and "[Y]ou keeping this?" are met with disinterest from a detached Billie who ultimately responds, "[T]ake what you like. I don't care" (Sears, 1997: 51), as they meditate on the subject matter represented by the books. "From man to mollusk. The scientific foundation for why we're not human" (51), Billie says, summarizing the content of the books on their bookshelf as Shakespeare interrupts her thoughts: "In genetics, or the study of what's wrong with people of African descent – The Heritage Foundation will give you tons of dough to prove the innate inferiority of . . . The Shakespeare's mine, but you can have it" (52). While this redistribution of intellectual property might seem unremarkable on the surface, the context and timing of this scene draws upon significant ideas about race, racism, and racial formation – from its historical roots to its present iterations.

Othello's and Billie's conversation is situated in an intimate and challenging moment; the separation of textual material that commingled on the bookshelves they once shared represents the dissolution of their relationship, which ended because of their disparate and diverging beliefs about Black life and social progress (Mehdizadeh, 2020: 17). Othello and Billie simply cannot see eye-to-eye, and this incompatibility has put an irreparable strain on their partnership. The central problem they face is that Othello believes that too much focus on racial injustice has led to more oppression for Black people. He is "tired of this race shit" (Sears, 1997: 55) and longs for a world more concerned with his talent than his race. His sentiment comes on the heels of his academic appointment, specifically his leadership position in managing his department's summer courses in Cyprus. The appointment is contentious because Othello was in competition for the position with his colleague, Chris Yago, and he admits that some of his colleagues "think I'm only there because I'm Black. I've tested it" (53). Thus, rather than objecting to white racism, Othello chooses to blame a policy (Affirmative Action) that attempts to redress racial injustice, despite describing specific instances in which his white colleagues disregard and disempower his intellectual and professional contributions to the department. It is easier to blame the policy rather than the white institution at which he wants to be at home. Whether or not Affirmative Action helped him secure his position, to him and his white colleagues, its existence implies that he required accommodations while his white counterparts seemingly succeeded on merit.

Othello's confession revisits the professional origins of Iago's spite toward Othello in Shakespeare's play, because Iago was sidelined for promotion by the usurpation of Cassio, whom he deemed unqualified.

This is, of course, not the only reason for Iago's hatred toward Othello, who promoted Cassio; his statement, "I hate the Moor" (1.3.369) is supported throughout the play as he enumerates the many reasons for his contempt. Racism, however, is the unstated motivation that haunts his every action. As we have discussed, Iago's reminders of Othello's Blackness, his sexualization of Othello's body, and his determination to destroy Othello's life, are all rooted in his belief that his Black counterpart is beneath him and undeserving of the Venetian life he is trying to build. Though Othello desires to be in community with the Venetian citizens, and though he holds a leadership position meant to protect them, he will never be considered an equal, a truth that the repeated racist epithets in the play confirm. Sears's revisitation of this moment in the present-day conversation between Othello and Billie reminds readers of the white racial hierarchy and the white racial frame that structures social relations. A policy like Affirmative Action attempts to create equity in an unjust system, but when those in power do not perceive the system as unjust because they are racist or lack racial literacy to decipher it, they will continue to frame corrective measures as unearned accommodations for people they perceive as inferior.

While Othello yearns for a world where race has no meaning, one where he will be unconditionally accepted by his white colleagues, Billie believes that such a world can never exist. She holds that the past will always bear upon the present, and histories of anti-Black racism like Arthur Lovejoy's *The Great Chain of Being* (1936) will regulate Black life. Lovejoy argues that everything on earth is hierarchized, from that which is closest to God to the basest form of life. His philosophy became a tool for white supremacy, which uses race to hierarchize human identity, creating knowledge systems that supposedly confirmed the inferiority of non-whites, thereby justifying their oppression. As we have mapped out in *Anti-Racist Shakespeare*, Shakespeare's works also participate in such schemes, which Sears conjures with Othello and Billie. When Billie says, "The Heritage Foundation will give you tons of dough to prove the innate inferiority of ... The Shakespeare's mine, but you can have it" (Sears, 1997: 52), she identifies Shakespeare as another author among those she peruses on their bookshelf, whose works have denigrated Black life.

Though Billie initially claims him as hers, she rejects his ideas when she rejects her copy of his writing, and roots herself, instead, in her community. As Joyce Green MacDonald argues,

> [t]o discount this connection between oneself and one's memory community is a potentially serious matter, since misremembering or entirely forgetting the significance your community attached to its own sites of memory might be a sign of something greater than merely not understanding the past. It might also mean that a person had lost his place in the present, his ability to remember who he is and where he fits into an ordered society of like-minded friends, neighbors, and citizens. (MacDonald, 2020: 124)

In Billie's eyes, Othello's resistance to the past disconnects him from his present and forecloses the possibility of their future together. Her fears are not misplaced; she is reduced to a passing reference in Shakespeare's *Othello*, which anachronistically follows the unfolding of events that occur in Sears's prelude. In Shakespeare, the sybil is simply a memory from Othello's past that wreaks destruction on his present through the handkerchief. By rejecting Shakespeare in this moment from *Harlem Duet*, Billie rejects Shakespeare's erasure of Black history and his construction of Black identity. Sears repurposes Shakespeare to offer a narrative that speaks to Black women's experiences under white supremacy. What is salient for her in Shakespeare's *Othello* is the marginalized and absent presence of Black women who circulate on the fringes of Shakespeare's play. Sears recovers those women from Shakespeare's grip and sets them free by telling their stories from her perspective. Racial literacy is one of the necessary tools to understand Sears's *Harlem Duet*; without it, her "rhapsodic blues tragedy" (Sears, 1997: 14) remains as opaque as the sybil's sorcery. Sears's engagement with *Othello* demonstrates that Shakespeare can be repositioned so that other voices can be heard. Likewise, the pedagogy we advance in *Anti-Racist Shakespeare* encourages our students to dialogue with Shakespeare through practices of embodiment that hone their racial literacy skills and highlight what is salient to them in these works.

Teaching Vignette

Make Your Own Shakespeare

To provide students with an opportunity to apply their developing racial literacy skills, our three-part assignment called "Make Your Own Shakespeare" allows students to showcase their knowledge of Shakespeare and race according to what is salient to them. "Make Your Own Shakespeare" asks students to craft an adaptation concept for one of the plays assigned on the syllabus. Students write a rationale supporting their creative choices using textual evidence, rewrite a scene from their chosen play according to their vision, and create a poster, playbill, or advertisement of their adaptation geared toward their intended audience that expresses the major themes that animate their adaptation. This assignment is designed for students to create with and through Shakespeare in order to unsettle the positioning of Shakespeare's texts as sacred objects. One of the purposes of this assignment is to encourage student engagement with the texts by treating them as the performance scripts they are, while emphasizing salience, adaptation, and embodiment. Students have the freedom to play with and remake Shakespeare so that the texts serve their intellectual interests and creative explorations. The project relies on critical thinking because students explain their adaptation through a thesis-driven rationale as well as a public-facing activity that renders salient the themes they want to communicate to their intended audience. Some may argue that such an approach takes the academic study of Shakespeare far afield from its original context, that ceding authority to students and to what is salient to them is not "real Shakespeare." To these skeptics, we respond by reiterating that embodiment and adaptation must reflect a thorough knowledge of Shakespeare to be convincing. Moreover, we task students with exhibiting their deep knowledge of the material in an intellectually rigorous and persuasive way, which means they must have fluency in and command of the material.

In developing their adaptations through "Make Your Own Shakespeare," students will reflect on the qualities, ideas, and themes that are salient to them in their chosen text. Moreover, because this assignment is developed in the context of an anti-racist Shakespeare course, attention to race should be prioritized, in terms of characters, setting, and with regard to students' intended audiences and communities. We argue that this multi-faceted project gives students the opportunity to showcase the skills they learned in the course and to be creative in their explorations, giving them more agency to guide their own learning with the support of the classroom community and instructor feedback.

The first part of "Make Your Own Shakespeare" is the rationale. In the rationale, students communicate the concept of their adaptation, which will address one or two tensions they want to bring into particular focus and that inform the action of the entire play. Examples of these tensions include: rule/misrule, duty/desire, and honor/infamy. This framework allows students to explore what is salient to them while anchoring the arguments and claims they seek to make through their adaptation in textual evidence and close readings. Adaptations can take several forms, including a theatrical or cinematic performance, a novel, short-story, non-fiction, memoir, music video, short film, narrative poem, or a painting, to give a few examples. Regardless of the form, the rationale should include detailed information about their concept, such as the setting of their adaptation, costume and set design, as well as any musical choices that can help them ground their adaptation in a particular locale.

The second component of "Make Your Own Shakespeare" is the rewrite. In this section, students will exhibit the vision and argument of their adaptation by rewriting no more than one or two scenes from their chosen play. Because the form of the adaptation will be different for each student, we recommend flexibility in how students approach their scene selection. We also recommend that instructors encourage students to untether the adaptation from Shakespeare's language and to support students in the creative process. With this freedom, students can explore various kinds of rewrites that can include writing primarily in prose, transforming a scene into visual art or music, working within different linguistic traditions, or other creative approaches. What we emphasize in our classrooms is that whatever method they choose, and however they choose to compose their rewrites, their adaptation should be reflective of their rationale (or if they find that the creative process led them toward a different path, they should revisit and revise the rationale to offer support for their choices). These varied modalities are expansive ways of generating new meanings from Shakespeare's texts with attention to society, culture, and social location.

The third component of "Make Your Own Shakespeare" is the poster, playbill, or advertisement. The main purpose of this component of the assignment is to help students learn how to translate themes from Shakespeare's works that are salient to them – which they highlight in their adaptation – into a public-facing context. This activity teaches students how to frame their positions depending on their target audience, which is necessary in their development as critical thinkers and writers. When students identify their intended audience, they can create a poster, playbill, or advertisement that specifically compels their audience to engage with their vision. The artifact that they create should also reflect the rationale and the rewrite, communicating the project's argument in an accessible way. Because racial literacy has been a vital component of the course, the poster, playbill, or advertisement should be attentive to race as it relates the themes of the adaptation, which they can ensure with the support of their instructor.

"Make Your Own Shakespeare" is designed to prioritize students' voices as they critically engage with and through Shakespeare. Their projects demonstrate how and why Shakespeare has had such longevity, which is because his works can be remade. As we explain to our students, his plays are only alive because people keep picking them up and playing with them.

Teacher Reflection

We end each section by asking teachers to reflect on their pedagogy as it relates to the topic of the section. In this section, we advocate that teachers develop Shakespeare pedagogy based on what is salient to students. We argue that this critically informed process produces an understanding of his works and bolsters racial literacy, providing students with a framework to interpret how race functions inside and outside of the classroom. For this "Teacher Reflection," we invite you to consider Shakespeare's salience in your pedagogy:

- How does Shakespeare's cultural capital inform how you approach your teaching?
- How will prioritizing salience over relevance impact your Shakespeare pedagogy?
- What concerns you about granting agency to students to find what is salient to them?
- Many of your students will find salience in different aspects of Shakespeare; how will you navigate those differences and still be supportive of their individual processes?
- What lasting effect do you hope this reorientation to Shakespeare will have on your students?

These reflective questions about salience and racial literacy are meant to help teachers consider how subjectivity informs what becomes salient in Shakespeare. By responding to these questions, whether in solitude or in community with others, in written, oral, or conceptual formats, teachers may feel discomfort about destabilizing formal methods of interpreting Shakespeare's works. We hope that creating this reflective space for teachers motivates them to create new course activities that support students' creativity and develop their racial literacy even as teachers discover new ways for Shakespeare to become salient for them.

Conclusion: The Ongoing Work of Anti-Racist Shakespeares

In *Anti-Racist Shakespeare*, we have argued that the Shakespeare classroom is an exemplary site for transformative, anti-racist pedagogy. Shakespeare's oeuvre engages with multiple and layered systems of power, such as race, gender, class, religion, and sexuality, and the varied interest of his plays in either interrogating or upholding those systems facilitate investigations that expose the process of racial formation in conjunction with other hierarchies of domination. Thus, the anti-racist work we advocate for in the classroom offers students an opportunity to understand the *longue durée* of racial formation, to investigate the intersection of race with other forms of power, and to intervene in these discourses and systems through their new critical perspectives. Throughout this Element we have offered theories, methods, and strategies for inclusive anti-racist pedagogy, ranging from course development to classroom practices that will facilitate critical engagement with issues of race, racism, and racial formation on syllabi, in texts, and between students. Because we are committed to transformative pedagogy with our own students, we have shared techniques that build capacity within instructors and students to create and cultivate knowledge through rigorous intellectual practices and respect for each other's different experiences, social locations, and humanity.

Effective anti-racist pedagogy begins with establishing a foundation grounded in collaboration and compassion, creating transformative spaces for knowledge production. As we have outlined, this transformation begins with instructors. If instructors are earnest about cultivating an anti-racist pedagogy, they will dedicate time to immersing themselves in resources that will provide them with the tools to support their students in their learning. This process requires a robust, multi-faceted comprehension of race and the operations of white supremacy. As we have demonstrated, whiteness has historically been an obscured category in the analysis of race in Shakespeare's works; yet Shakespeare's whiteness informs his construction of imaginary worlds. Developing racial literacy, therefore, is necessary to build a critical orientation that fully grasps how race works in Shakespeare's texts. Racial literacy is a tool that helps instructors and students untangle the complexity of race, by decoding the overt and covert language of race in white supremacist societies. It assists instructors in their course design, reading selections, and assignment construction and helps them become more aware of who they are including or excluding in every stage of course development. Through this instruction, students can then make connections with the literature in their daily lives because their instructors have created the space to do this work.

Our suggestion to create, implement, and reinforce Community Norms as guides for student interaction during the term can aid instructors and students in tackling difficult conversations about race, which is critical to develop and sustain an anti-racist classroom. When students feel like they are an integral part of the course, they are more likely to invest in the collective work of the class, and therefore more likely to deepen their understanding of Shakespeare to discover what is salient to them. Salience is a key concept in *Anti-Racist Shakespeare*, one that empowers students because it does not expect them to automatically relate to Shakespeare, his genius, and his universality. Rather, salience emphasizes students' interests, experiences, and intellectual investments as they engage with Shakespeare's texts. Salience can be a critical tool in cultivating an anti-racist pedagogy because it highlights the knowledge that students bring to their intellectual inquiry while also revealing new avenues for interpreting the race-work in which Shakespeare's texts are engaged. In tandem with racial literacy, salience disrupts the quotidian operations of racism by enacting the ethical commitments of anti-racism.

At the end of each section of this Element, we have given instructors a glimpse into some of our teaching practices through our Teaching Vignettes and have offered them the opportunity to reflect on the theories, methods, and strategies that we have shared through Teaching Reflections. These are open-ended invitations to interact with this Element, its arguments, positions, and approaches. Our orientation throughout this Element has been to advance anti-racist pedagogy through theory, practice, and action, and we encourage our readers to adopt, develop, and expand our work according to their anti-racist pedagogical commitments. While our focus has been on Shakespeare because we are both early modern scholars, our intention with *Anti-Racist Shakespeare* has been to share theories, methodologies, and strategies that can be adapted and applied more broadly. Therefore, we hope that this Element will help readers cultivate, develop, or maintain anti-racist pedagogy in any classroom.

While many of our recommendations and techniques align with in-person instructional formats, we conceptualized and wrote much of this Element during the height of the COVID-19 global pandemic when most academic instruction transferred to online platforms. Thus, we invite readers to consider how the approaches we outline in *Anti-Racist Shakespeare* can be amended to a variety of teaching contexts, and to reformulate and tailor our work to suit these needs. We do not conceive of *Anti-Racist Shakespeare* as a rigid set of components and policies; rather, we encourage adaptation and experimentation to meet the exigencies of a diverse array of institutions, instructors, and students. As we state at the beginning of this Element, our study is part of an ongoing scholarly conversation in PCRS and Shakespeare studies, and our emphasis is on the critical insights that can happen in the classroom. We do not presume to have the last word on Shakespeare or anti-racist pedagogy. In fact, we hope that there will be much more to come because the world we live in requires a collective commitment to abolishing harmful systems of domination and subordination. Anti-racism is vital to creating a just and "brave new world."

Bibliography

Aceshowbiz (2020). "During a Zoom Call with the Media after Winning an Emmy." Aceshowbiz. www.aceshowbiz.com/news/view/00160065.html [Accessed 3/26/2022].

Adams, B. (2021). "Fair/Foul." In C. L. Bourne, ed., *Shakespeare/Text: Contemporary Readings in Textual Studies*. New York: Arden, pp. 29–49.

Ahmed, S. (2006). *Queer Phenomenology*. Durham: Duke University Press.

Akhimie, P. (2020). "'Fair' Bianca and 'Brown' Kate: Shakespeare and the Mixed-Race Family in José Esquea's *The Taming of the Shrew*." *Journal of American Studies*, 54(1), 89–96.

Anderson, N. (2015). "Skipping Shakespeare? Yes, English Majors Can Often Bypass the Bard." *Washington Post*. April 23. www.washington post.com/news/grade-point/wp/2015/04/23/skipping-shakespeare-yes-english-majors-can-often-bypass-the-bard/ [Accessed 8/2/2022].

Applebaum, B. (2010). *Being White, Being Good: White Complicity, White Moral Responsibility, and Social Justice Pedagogy*. New York: Lexington Books.

Applebaum, B. (2019). "White Ignorance, Epistemic Injustice and the Challenges of Teaching for Critical Social Consciousness." In G. Yancy, ed., *Educating for Critical Consciousness*. New York: Routledge, pp. 28–44.

Arao, B. & Clemens, K. (2013). "From Save Spaces to Brave Spaces: A New Way to Frame Dialogue around Diversity and Social Justice." Sterling: Stylus Publishing.

Arnold, M. (1869). *Culture and Anarchy*, ed. J. Garnett. New York: Oxford World Classics.

Barthelemy, A. G. (1999). *Black Face, Maligned Race: The Representation of Blacks in English Drama from Shakespeare to Southerne*. Baton Rouge: Louisiana State University Press.

Bell, D. (1995). "Who's Afraid of Critical Race Theory." *University of Illinois Law Review*, 1995(4), 893–910.

Blake, F. (2019). "Why Black Lives Matter in the Humanities." In K. Crenshaw, G. Lipsitz, L. Charles Harris, and D. HoSang, eds., *Seeing Race Again: Countering Colorblindness Across the Disciplines*. Berkeley: University of California Press, pp. 307–26.

Bonilla-Silva, E. (2006). *Racism without Racists: Color-Blind Racism and the Persistence of Racial Inequality in the United States*. New York: Rowman & Littlefield Publishers.

Boster, T. (2019). "From Pansophia to Public Humanities: Connecting Past and Present Through Community-Based Learning." In H. Eklund and W. B. Hyman, eds., *Teaching Social Justice Through Shakespeare: Why Renaissance Literature Matters Now*. Edinburgh: Edinburgh University Press, pp. 215–24.

Britton, D. (2018). "Ain't She a Shakespearean: Truth, Giovanni, and Shakespeare." In C. L. Smith, N. R. Jones, and M. Grier, eds., *Early Modern Black Diaspora Studies*. New York: Palgrave Macmillan, pp. 223–28.

Colchester, M. (2022). "Inside Boris Johnson's Partygate Scandal." *The Wall Street Journal*. February 10. www.wsj.com/articles/boris-johnson-partygate-scandal-uk-politics-11644508593 [Accessed 24/3/2022].

Collins, P. H. (2019). *Intersectionality as Critical Social Theory*. Durham, NC: Duke University Press.

Corredera, V. I. (2017). "Far More Black Than Black: Stereotypes, Black Masculinity, and Americanization in Tim Blake Nelson's O." *Literary / Film Quarterly*. 45(3), https://lfq.salisbury.edu/_issues/45_3/far_more_black_than_black.html [Accessed 3/27/2022].

Corredera, V. I. (2020). "'How Dey Goin' to Kill Othello?!' *Key & Peele* and Shakespearean Universality." *Journal of American Studies*, 54(1), 27–35.

Crenshaw, K. W., ed. (2019). *Seeing Race Again: Countering Colorblindness across the Disciplines*. Berkeley: University of California Press.

Dadabhoy, A. (2020a). "Skin in the Game: Teaching Race in Early Modern Literature." *Studies in Medieval and Renaissance Teaching*, 27(2), 1–17.

Dadabhoy, A. (2020b). "The Unbearable Whiteness of Being (in) Shakespeare." *Postmedieval*, 11, 228–35.

Dadabhoy, A. (2021). "Barbarian Moors: Documenting Racial Formation in Early Modern England." In A. Thompson, ed., *The Cambridge Companion to Shakespeare and Race*. Cambridge: Cambridge University Press, pp. 30–46.

De Barros, E. L. (2019). ""Shakespeare" on His Lips': Dreaming of the Shakespeare Center for Radical Thought and Transformative Action." In H. Eklund and W. B. Hyman, eds., *Teaching Social Justice Through Shakespeare: Why Renaissance Literature Matters Now*. Edinburgh: Edinburgh University Press, pp. 206–14.

Dyer, R. (2017). *White: Essays on Race and Culture*. New York: Routledge.

Eklund, H. & Hyman, W. B., eds. (2019). *Teaching Social Justice Through Shakespeare: Why Renaissance Literature Matters Now*. Edinburgh: Edinburgh University Press.

Erickson, P. (2013). "'Late Has No Meaning Here': Imagining a Second Chance in Toni Morrison's Desdemona." *Borrowers and Lenders: The Journal of Shakespeare and Appropriation*, 8(1). www.proquest.com/docview/1458231644.

Erickson, P. and Hall, K. F. (2016). "'A New Scholarly Song': Rereading Early Modern Race." *Shakespeare Quarterly*, 67(1), 1–13.

Espinosa, R. (2016). "Stranger Shakespeare." *Shakespeare Quarterly*, 67(1), 51–67.

Fanon, F. (2008). *Black Skin, White Masks*. London: Pluto Press.

Feagin, J. R. (2006). *Systemic Racism: A Theory of Oppression*. New York: Routledge.

Feagin, J. R. (2020). *The White Racial Frame: Centuries of Racial Framing and Counter-Framing*. New York: Routledge.

Fields, K. E. and Fields, B. J. (2014). *Racecraft: The Soul of Inequality in American Life*. New York: Verso Books.

Flensner, K. K. and Von der Lippe, M. (2019). "Being Safe from What and Safe for Whom? A Critical Discussion of the Conceptual Metaphor of 'Safe Space.'" *Intercultural Education*, 30(3), 275–88.

Freire, P. (1970). *Pedagogy of the Oppressed*, trans. M. B. Ramos. New York: Continuum International Publishing Group.

Grier, M. P. (2018). "The Color of Professionalism: A Response to Dennis Britton." In C. Smith, N. Jones, and M. Grier, eds., *Early Modern Black Diaspora Studies: A Critical Anthology*. New York: Palgrave-MacMillan, pp. 229–38.

Gunia, A., Nugent C., Moon, K. et al. (2021). "The Racial Reckoning Went Global Last Year: Here's How Activists in 8 Countries Are Fighting for Justice." *Time*. May 11. https://time.com/6046299/fighting-injustice-world/ [Accessed 3/26/2022].

Hall, K. F. (1995). *Things of Darkness: Economies of Race and Gender in Early Modern England*. Ithaca, NY: Cornell University Press.

Hall, K. F. (1996). "Beauty and the Beast of Whiteness: Teaching Race and Gender." *Shakespeare Quarterly*, 47(4), 461–75.

Hall, S. (2021a). "Teaching Race." In *Selected Writings on Race and Difference*. Durham, NC: Duke University Press, pp. 123–35.

Hall, S. (2021b). "Race, the Floating Signifier: What More Is There to Say about 'Race'?" In *Selected Writings on Race and Difference*. Durham, NC: Duke University Press, pp. 359–73.

Hendricks, M. (2019). "Coloring the Past, Rewriting Our Future: RaceB4Race." Folger Shakespeare Library. www.folger.edu/institute/scholarly-programs/race-periodization/margo-hendricks [Accessed 3/27/2022].

Holloway, K. (2021). "Here's What 'Succession' Gets So Right About Toxic Whiteness." *Daily Beast*. November 28. www.thedailybeast.com/heres-what-succession-gets-so-right-about-toxic-whiteness [Accessed 3/26/22].

hooks, b. (1992). *Black Looks: Race and Representation*. Boston, MA: South End Press.

hooks, b. (1994). *Teaching to Transgress: Education as the Practice of Freedom*. New York: Routledge.

Kaplan, M. Lindsay. "Jessica's Mother: Medieval Constructions of Jewish Race and Gender in" The Merchant of Venice"." *Shakespeare Quarterly* 58, no. 1 (2007): 1–30.

Kaplan, M. Lindsay. *Figuring racism in medieval Christianity*. Oxford University Press, USA, 2018.

Kidnie, M. J. (2008). *Shakespeare and the Problem of Adaptation*. New York: Routledge.

Kishimoto, K. (2018). "Anti-Racist Pedagogy: From Faculty's Self-Reflection to Organizing within and beyond the Classroom." *Race Ethnicity and Education*, 21(4), 540–54.

MacDonald, J. G. (2020). *Shakespearean Adaptation, Race and Memory in the New World*. New York: Palgrave Macmillan.

Medina, J. (2017). "Epistemic Injustice and Epistemologies of Ignorance." In P. Taylor, L. Alcoff, and L. Anderson, eds., *The Routledge Companion to Philosophy of Race*. New York: Routledge.

Mehdizadeh, N. (2020). "Othello in Harlem: Transforming Theater in Djanet Sears' *Harlem Duet*." In "Shakespeare and Black America," ed. P. Cahill and K. F. Hall, special issue, *Journal of American Studies*, 54(1), 12–18.

Mehdizadeh, N. (in press). "'In Her Prophetic Fury': Teaching Critical Modes of Intervention in Shakespeare Studies." In ed. Patricia Akhimie, *The Oxford Handbook of Shakespeare and Race*. New York: Oxford University Press.

Mejia LaPerle, C. (2022). *Race and Affect: In Early Modern English Literature*. Tempe: ACMRS Press. https://asu.pressbooks.pub/race-and-affect/front-matter/introduction/ [Accessed 3/30/2022].

Mendoza, K. N. (2019). "Sexual Violence, Trigger Warnings, and the Early Modern Classroom." In H. Eklund and W. B. Hyman, eds., *Teaching*

Social Justice Through Shakespeare: Why Renaissance Literature Matters Now. Edinburgh: Edinburgh University Press, pp. 97–105.

Mills, C. W. (1997). *The Racial Contract*. Ithaca: Cornell University Press.

Mills, C. W. (1998). *Blackness Visible*. Ithaca: Cornell University Press.

Mills, C. W. (2003). "White Supremacy as Sociopolitical System: A Philosophical Perspective." In A. W. Doane and E. Bonilla-Silva, eds., *White Out*. New York: Routledge, pp. 42–55.

Morrison, T. (2019). *The Source of Self-Regard: Selected Essays, Speeches, and Meditations*. New York: Knopf.

Newman-Bremang, K. (2021). "Of Course *Succession* Fails Its Black Women Characters – It's *Succession*." *Refinery29*. December 6. www.refinery29.com/en-us/2021/12/10785227/succession-black-characters-season-3-review [Accessed 3/26/2022].

Nieto, S. (2010). *Language, Culture, and Teaching: Critical Perspectives*. New York: Routledge.

Okri, B. (2015). *A Way of Being Free*. London: Orion.

Omi, M. and Winant, H. (2014). *Racial Formation in the United States*. New York: Routledge.

Pittman, L. M. (2011). *Authorizing Shakespeare on Film and Television: Gender, Class, and Ethnicity in Adaptation*. Studies in Shakespeare 19. New York: Peter Lang Publishing.

Royster, F. T. (2000). "White-Limed Walls: Whiteness and Gothic Extremism in Shakespeare's *Titus Andronicus*." *Shakespeare Quarterly*, 51(4), 432–55.

Ruby, M. (2020). "Tokenism." In Z. A. Casey, ed., *Encyclopedia of Critical Whiteness Studies in Education*. New York: Brill, pp. 675–80.

Said, E. (2003). *Orientalism*. New York: Penguin.

Sanchez Castillo, M. (2019). "Blackness in Shakespeare's Works: English Professor Ian Smith Discusses Class on Dispelling 'Racial Blind Spots.'"

The Lafayette. March 1. https://lafayettestudentnews.com/64312/arts/draft-teaching-race-in-shakespeare-english-professor-ian-smith-talks-about-racial-blind-spots-in-shakespearean-literature/ [Accessed 26/3/2022].

Sealey-Ruiz, Y. (2020). *Racial Literacy: A Policy Research Brief*. Champaign: National Council of Teachers of English. https://ncte.org/wp-content/uploads/2021/04/SquireOfficePolicyBrief_RacialLiteracy_April2021.pdf [Accessed 8/5/2022].

Sears, D. (1997). *Harlem Duet*. Toronto: Scirocco Drama.

Sears, D. (2004). "An Interview with Djanet Sears," interview by Mat Buntin. *Canadian Adaptations Shakespeare Project*. https://web.archive.org/web/20200115134616/www.canadianshakespeares.ca/i_dsears.cfm [Accessed 3/2/2022].

Shakespeare, W. (2000). *Titus Andronicus*, ed. R. McDonald. New York: Penguin.

Shakespeare, W. (2007). *Othello, the Moor of Venice: Texts and Contexts*, ed. K. F. Hall. New York: Bedford/St. Martin's Press.

Shakespeare, W. (2008). *As You Like It*, ed. A. Brissenden. New York: Oxford: Oxford University Press.

Shakespeare, W. (2009). *Hamlet*, ed. B. A. Mowat & P. Werstine. New York: Folger Shakespeare Library.

Shakespeare, W. (2017). *Henry V*, ed. C. McEchearn. New York: Penguin.

Smith, I. (2013). "Othello's Black Handkerchief." *Shakespeare Quarterly*, 64(1), 1–25.

Smith, I. (2020). "Whiteness: A Primer for Understanding Shakespeare." YouTube video. Folger Shakespeare Library. www.youtube.com/watch?v=WsD0DNk-0Oo [Accessed 24/3/ 2022].

Summers, J. J. and Svinicki, M. D. (2007). "Investigating Classroom Community in Higher Education." *Learning and Individual Differences*, 17(1), 55–67.

Tatum, B. D. (1992). "Talking about Race, Learning about Racism: The Application of Racial Identity Development Theory in the Classroom." *Harvard Educational Review*, 62(1), 1–25.

Tatum, B. D. (2017). *Why Are All the Black Kids Sitting Together in the Cafeteria*. New York: Basic Books.

Thiong'o, N. (2005). *Decolonizing the Mind: The Politics of Language and African Literature*. New York: James Currey.

Thompson, A. and Turchi, L. (2016). *Teaching Shakespeare with a Purpose: A Student-Centered Approach*. London: Bloomsbury.

Thompson, A. (2019). "An Afterword About Self/Communal Care." In H. Eklund and W. B. Hyman, eds., *Teaching Social Justice Through Shakespeare: Why Renaissance Literature Matters Now*. Edinburgh: Edinburgh University Press, pp. 235–38.

Turner, C. (2021). "'White Privilege' Should Not Be Taught In Schools." *The Telegraph*. October 21. www.telegraph.co.uk/news/2021/10/21/white-privilege-should-not-taught-schools-fact-says-nadhim-zahawi/ [Accessed 3/26/2022].

Twine, F. W. (2011). *A White Side of Black Britain: Interracial Intimacy and Racial Literacy*. Durham, NC: Duke University Press.

Viswanathan, G. (2014). *Masks of Conquest: Literary Study and British Rule in India*. New York: Columbia University Press.

Wilcock, D. (2022). "Boris Johnson Stokes Dominick Cummings Row." *The Daily Mail*. February 1. www.dailymail.co.uk/news/article-10463393/Boris-Johnson-stokes-Dominic-Cummings-row-comparing-relationship-Othello-Iago.html [Accessed 3/26/2022].

Wise, D. (2021). "*Succession's* Jesse Armstrong On The Dangers Of Creating Unsavoury Characters: 'You Have To Be Careful.'" *Deadline*. October 16. https://deadline.com/2021/10/successions-jesse-armstrong-dangers-of-creating-unsavoury-characters-you-have-to-be-careful-lff-1234856924/ [Accessed 3/26/2022].

Acknowledgments

Every scholarly project accrues many debts, and our debt is to our intellectual scholarly community, friends, families (including our pets!), and, of course, our students from whom we learn every day. We want to thank everyone who has supported our scholarship, which has allowed us to contribute to the ongoing conversation about anti-racist pedagogy. We especially want to express our gratitude to our various collaborators and interlocutors whose generosity has enriched our thinking and enhanced the vision of our Element.

Dedication

For our students, teachers, communities, and families

Cambridge Elements ☰

Elements in Shakespeare and Pedagogy

Liam E. Semler
University of Sydney

Liam E. Semler is Professor of Early Modern Literature in the Department of English at the University of Sydney. He is author of Teaching Shakespeare and Marlowe: Learning versus the System (2013) and co-editor (with Kate Flaherty and Penny Gay) of Teaching Shakespeare beyond the Centre: Australasian Perspectives (2013). He is editor of Coriolanus: A Critical Reader (2021) and co-editor (with Claire Hansen and Jackie Manuel) of Reimagining Shakespeare Education: Teaching and Learning through Collaboration (Cambridge, forthcoming). His most recent book outside Shakespeare studies is The Early Modern Grotesque: English Sources and Documents 1500–1700 (2019). Liam leads the Better Strangers project which is a collaborative, Shakespeare education partnership between the University of Sydney and Sydney school Barker College. Better Strangers hosts the open-access Shakespeare Reloaded website (shakespearereloaded.edu.au).

Gillian Woods
Birkbeck College, University of London

Gillian Woods is Reader in Renaissance Literature and Theatre at Birkbeck College, University of London. She is the author of Shakespeare's Unreformed Fictions (2013; joint winner of Shakespeare's Globe Book Award), Romeo and Juliet: A Reader's Guide to Essential Criticism (2012), and numerous articles about Renaissance drama. She is the co-editor (with Sarah Dustagheer) of Stage Directions and Shakespearean Theatre (2018). She is currently working on an updated edition of A Midsummer Night's Dream for Cambridge University Press, as well as a Leverhulme-funded monograph about Renaissance Theatricalities. As founding director of the Shakespeare Teachers' Conversations, she runs a seminar series that brings together university academics, school teachers and educationalists from non-traditional sectors, and she regularly runs workshops for schools.

ABOUT THE SERIES

The teaching and learning of Shakespeare around the world is complex and changing. Elements in Shakespeare and Pedagogy synthesises theory and practice, including provocative, original pieces of research, as well as dynamic, practical engagements with learning contexts.

Cambridge Elements ☰

Elements in Shakespeare and Pedagogy